Advance Praise for *Warrior Mom* by JJ Virgin
(Previously published as *Miracle Mindset*)

"So many of us live in fear of something terrible happening to one of our loved ones and wonder if we'd find the strength to survive in the face of tragedy. JJ faced the unimaginable with her son with grace and bravery, and in *Miracle Mindset* she shows how each of us can tap into our hidden strength when we need it most."

—Patty Aubery, coauthor of *Chicken Soup for the Christian Soul* and
president of Jack Canfield Companies

"In *Miracle Mindset*, JJ shares a side of herself that her readers haven't seen before—vulnerable, brave, and yet wholly relatable. Mothers will see themselves in JJ as she fights for her son's life, and readers will gain strength from JJ as they watch her do the impossible. This book is about facing your worst nightmare with courage, faith, and forgiveness. JJ Virgin isn't afraid to tell you the truth about her own hard times and how she got through them."

—Sara Gottfried, MD, *New York Times* bestselling author of
The Hormone Cure and *The Hormone Reset Diet*

"What would you do if you weren't afraid? As someone who has faced numerous adversities in my life, not knowing where I would get the strength or courage to make it through, JJ's words from *Miracle Mindset* are the ones I wished someone had said to me. JJ has inspired me to stay strong, take more chances, and show up in my own life. Everyone should read this book!"

—Cynthia Pasquella-Garcia, founder of
the Institute of Transformational Nutrition

"Chances are you will experience trauma in your life. There's good news—you don't have to be held back by what happened to you. There IS another way. JJ Virgin's *Miracle Mindset* is a story of hope, inspiration, and paves a way to turn any trauma into power."

—Mastin Kipp, life interventionist and bestselling author

"*Miracle Mindset* is a book about tragedy and triumph, hard work, dedication, and a mother whose lifetime of service helped save her son from certain death. JJ Virgin shows exactly what it takes to step up in the hardest times and come out stronger."

—Daniel G. Amen, MD, founder of Amen Clinics and coauthor of
The Brain Warrior's Way

"In a time when so much of what we see and read can be discouraging, JJ Virgin is a reminder of the very best we human beings have to offer: honesty, strength, and the willingness to step up and fight for the people we love."

—Amy Myers, MD, author of *New York Times* bestsellers
The Thyroid Connection and *The Autoimmune Solution*

"We hear a lot about how the hardships we face in life make us stronger, and JJ Virgin proves this to be true. She teaches us that facing our challenges head-on brings out the best in us."

—Dean Graziosi, *New York Times* bestselling author and
America's Success Coach

"An inspiring, moving read that reminds us all what true strength looks like!"

—Lewis Howes, *New York Times* bestselling author of
The School of Greatness

"A remarkable story of resilience and love. What would you do if tragedy struck your family on the very same day your life's work was set to come to fruition? In *Miracle Mindset*, JJ Virgin shows us how to grow the courage to overcome anything life brings to your door."

—Dave Asprey, *New York Times* bestselling author of *The Bulletproof Diet*

"*Miracle Mindset* is riveting and powerful. It is a tale of a mother's unwillingness to give up on her child. The power of her stance makes the entire universe bend into a wonderful outcome. This book is a must-read with twists and turns that really make us think about life."

—Pedram Shojai, OMD, founder of Well.org and *New York Times* bestselling author of *The Urban Monk*

"So many books tell us to be strong in the face of adversity, but in *Miracle Mindset*, JJ Virgin shows us how."

—Darren Hardy, founding publisher and editor (emeritus) of *SUCCESS* magazine and *New York Times* bestselling author of *The Compound Effect*

"JJ faced the unimaginable with her son. She did it with grace and bravery, and in *Miracle Mindset* she shows how each of us can tap into our hidden strength when we need it most."

—Hal Elrod, #1 bestselling author of *The Miracle Morning*

"JJ Virgin is the most courageous person I know, and her courage is contagious. No matter what challenges you're facing, JJ's amazing story will inspire you to stay strong and hopeful—and her 'miracle mindset' will empower you to live a better, braver life."

—Dr. Kellyann Petrucci, *New York Times* bestselling author of *Dr. Kellyann's Bone Broth Diet* and DrKellyann.com, and host of the public television special *21 Days to a Slimmer, Younger You*

"*Miracle Mindset* is a story of tragedy and triumph and the road map for each one of us to follow in our own journey through tough times to a stronger and greater place in life and in ourselves. This is a book you not only read, this is a book you live. You will be so grateful for the gifts in this book that you will want to come back again and again."

—Mary Morrissey, world-renowned life coach, motivational speaker, spiritual author, and founder of the Life Mastery Institute

"Anything with JJ Virgin's name on it has my vote. She has changed the way I think of food, eating, and nutrition, and her ideas have added years to my life. But with this book, JJ reveals a whole new side of herself, and the story and lessons of the battles she went through to save a son's life and juggle a formidable career is filled with beautiful, empowering lessons for every person on the planet who has at any time felt like giving up amidst tragedy, or been unable to imagine how they could succeed despite overwhelming odds. This book will show you just how powerful love can be."

—Vishen Lakhiani, *New York Times* bestselling author of *The Code of the Extraordinary Mind* and CEO of Mindvalley

"I couldn't put *Miracle Mindset* down. I was completely transfixed by JJ's story and desperate to learn if she could possibly defy the odds in the face of seemingly insurmountable obstacles. When I finally closed the book I felt a tidal wave of relief wash over me—not just for JJ, but also for all of us who face our own challenges in life. Now whenever I am overwhelmed or scared, I find myself thinking, 'If JJ can do it, so can I.'"

—Janet Bray Attwood, *New York Times* bestselling author of *The Passion Test* and *Your Hidden Riches*

Warrior Mom

7 Steps to Bold, Brave Resilience

Previously published as *Miracle Mindset*

JJ Virgin

G

GALLERY BOOKS

NEW YORK   LONDON   TORONTO   SYDNEY   NEW DELHI

G

Gallery Books
An Imprint of Simon & Schuster, Inc.
1230 Avenue of the Americas
New York, NY 10020

First Gallery Books trade paperback edition May 2018
First North Star Way hardcover edition (previously published as *Miracle Mindset*)
February 2017

GALLERY BOOKS and colophon are trademarks of Simon & Schuster, Inc.

For information about special discounts for bulk purchases,
please contact Simon & Schuster Special Sales at 1-866-506-1949
or business@simonandschuster.com.

The Simon & Schuster Speakers Bureau can bring authors to your live event.
For more information or to book an event, contact the Simon & Schuster Speakers
Bureau at 1-866-248-3049 or visit our website at www.simonandschuster.com.

Manufactured in the United States of America

10 9 8 7 6 5 4 3 2 1

Library of Congress Cataloging-in-Publication Data is available.

ISBN 978-1-5011-2987-2
ISBN 978-1-5011-2988-9 (pbk)
ISBN 978-1-5011-2989-6 (ebook)

TO BRYCE AND GRANT:

you are my miracles.

The women whom I love and admire for their strength and grace did not get that way because [things] worked out. They got that way because [things] went wrong, and they handled it. They handled it in a thousand different ways on a thousand different days, but they handled it. Those women are my superheroes.

—ELIZABETH GILBERT

Contents

The Best Worst Year

On September 10, 2012, my sixteen-year-old son Grant was struck down by a hit-and-run driver while he was out walking, and was left for dead in the street.

I would have given anything in that moment to trade places with my son. I can close my eyes and still be standing there in the ICU, holding Grant's hand while he was in a coma, awaiting the surgery we were told he wouldn't survive, listening to the machines that were keeping him alive. He had a tube coming out of his head to manage the pressure from multiple brain bleeds, another out of his neck for his central line, and one from the wrist that wasn't bandaged. He had a torn aorta (which kills 90 percent of people immediately, by the way) and thirteen fractures, plus severe road rash. The entire right side of his body was basically skinned raw. I know I don't have to tell you what it feels like to see someone you love helpless like that. There is nothing more painful. It is shocking.

His father, John, and I were told he most likely wouldn't make it through the night and that we should let him go.

We were given no hope. We were told not to airlift him, that he wouldn't survive the airlift to the only hospital in the area that could possibly save his life.

We airlifted him.

We were told he wouldn't survive the surgery to repair his aorta.

He survived it.

We were told he would never wake up.

He woke up.

We were told he would never walk again due to the thirteen fractures and especially the crushed heel injury, which the doctors called a "game changer."

A year later, Grant was playing tennis and working out regularly, and was stronger than ever.

We were told he would never hear out of his right ear again.

He can hear.

We were told that if he ever woke up, he would be so severely brain-damaged that saving his life wouldn't have been worth it.

Today he is 85 percent back mentally and still improving every day.

For weeks while Grant was in a coma, I spent my days at the hospital, working next to his bedside. When this happened, I was about to launch my first big book and was in the middle of expanding my business. As a forty-nine-year-old single mother of two, I couldn't let work slide while I focused on taking care of Grant. I needed to be able to support my kids now more than ever. The medical bills were already piling up, and I wasn't going to let not having money stop me from giving my son whatever he needed when he woke up. While there were some people who encouraged me to focus on Grant and forget about work, success had never meant more to my family or to me. Showing up less just wasn't an option.

Grant's recovery from the traumatic brain injury has been difficult for our whole family. Grant had to relearn how to talk, how to walk, and how to do everything from tie his shoes to say his name. There was violence and mood swings. More than once his father, John, and I tried to wrestle from him handfuls of pills that he managed to swallow. I have a younger son named Bryce, whose life had suddenly changed as well.

This was the worst time of my life. I had almost lost my son. His life was never going to be the same. I hadn't had a single day in which I wasn't at the hospital watching my child fight for his life, seeing it affect my other son, feeling guilty while I was on the road for work, wrestling my son away from fights with nurses, crying in private, praying for something better, and trying to show up every day for the people who were looking to me to help them with their own problems. And I knew that more hard days were still around each corner. This wasn't behind us yet, and deep down I knew that it never really would be.

But I am the type of person who has to believe that I am going to turn the worst thing that ever could have happened to my son into the best thing that has ever happened to him. And sure enough, there were days of amazing progress that made the months following Grant's accident into the best ones of my life as well. My son was alive, we were together, and every small step forward gave me so much hope. The first time he squeezed my hand and fluttered his eyelashes. His first words: "I love you." The smiles. The amazing drawings. The workouts.

As Grant inched his way toward recovery, I began sharing our story with friends, business associates, and even followers on social media, and something amazing happened. One by one, they began telling me how much strength they'd drawn from the image of me working to launch my book from Grant's bedside in the ICU. People who were going through something similar with a loved one visited my Facebook page to find out what we were doing for Grant. Others who were facing smaller challenges or were simply looking for the courage to push further in their lives and careers used our example to start questioning authority, overcoming their self-doubts, and opening their minds to new possibilities. As a result, their lives had begun to transform.

Over and over, people asked me, "How did you do it?" The truth is, I didn't know. When Grant was in the hospital, I was operating on pure animal instinct. There was no time for me to stop and ask myself what I was doing or why, and I had no idea that our story could touch so many lives.

It wasn't until after Grant was back home that I slowly began to make sense of everything that had happened. As I talked to friends and business associates both publicly and in private to process what I'd been through, it struck me that a number of them had experienced trauma in their own lives. It's no coincidence that many of the people who had gone on to achieve great success had also been through devastating lows. The skills they needed to be successful were the same ones that had helped them persevere through tragedy, and vice versa.

I realized that without even being aware of it, when Grant was in the hospital, I'd been drawing on lessons I'd learned the hard way throughout my entire life. Using the same mindset and techniques that I'd used to face previous challenges, build my own business, and help hundreds of thousands of people lose weight and get healthier, I had not only survived the worst year of my life but had thrived. I was closer to my family than ever and my business was booming. Even better, I realized that I could teach other people those same skills and help them prepare for the best and worst that life has to offer. The lessons from Grant's accident were bigger than me. They could reach far and wide and have a positive impact on thousands of people. That idea was exciting.

My son made it. We all made it. During what should have been the worst year of my life—watching my teenage son battle to recover from a hit-and-run accident that left him in a coma and then fighting to reclaim his cognition and his life—I had somehow helped my son begin to rebuild his life, helped other people change their lives, and found a new sense of purpose in myself, in my work, and in my relationships with my family.

In the following pages, I'll share with you the seven lessons I learned during the hardest period of my life, lessons I relied on during the difficult times and that helped me discover and tap into my personal power and purpose. These lessons are universal; they're not unique to me. Whether you're trying to lose weight, build a better business, or bring a family member back from the brink of death, these lessons together create a mindset that will make you unstoppable.

I call this mindset that allows you to show up for life, even when it is hard, and do the work that leads to unbelievable results the Miracle Mindset. My son has it. My clients have it. And I am quite sure I can credit all my successes in life to my own belief that miracles do happen when we show up and do the work. In this book, I hope to give you the ability to discover and nurture the Miracle Mindset in your own life so you can realize life-changing power and purpose.

I have seen the Miracle Mindset manifested in the hundreds of thank-you notes I have received from people around the world who've changed their own lives in the face of some of life's toughest obstacles—depression, unemployment, illness, weight loss, and injuries. And I know that the Miracle Mindset will continue to sustain me when life surprises me with its worst.

I am grateful that my story has a happy, hopeful ending, but this is also a hard story to share. In ways, I am still working through some of the trauma of almost losing my son and watching him work so hard every day to reclaim the life he had barely started. It has taken four years for Grant, Bryce, John, and me to be ready to look back on this experience, and now it is time for me to share what I have taken away from it in the hopes that our story will help you face every obstacle in your life—big and small, life-threatening and life-affirming. I want our struggles and our successes to inspire you and offer the hope and strength you need to face your own.

If you have something that you think is holding you back from your dreams, if you find yourself having the worst day of your life or a bad year, or if you are living through the absolute unthinkable and it feels like no one could possibly believe in you, I hope our story gives you the courage and the inspiration to say, "I am going to make this the Best Worst Year." The Miracle Mindset could make all the difference.

1

I'm Not as Strong as You Think I Am

Grant was never an easy kid. From the time he was a six-month-old refusing to sleep in his crib, I knew I had my work cut out for me. The pediatrician told me to just leave him alone in his room and let him cry, and eventually he would fall asleep. That may have worked with other babies, but Grant always found a way to escalate the situation, crying louder and louder for up to six hours at a time until I couldn't take it anymore.

The one thing Grant always loved was being a big brother. Bryce was born when Grant was just one year old. When Grant came to the hospital to meet his new brother for the first time, he suddenly looked so big. Really, he was still just a baby himself. But Grant took one look at Bryce sleeping in his little bassinet and handed him his beloved pacifier as a welcome gift. My heart just about melted.

Once we brought Bryce home, Grant's challenges became more apparent. Bryce had a calm, easygoing disposition. Instead of escalating things, Bryce always found a way to make life easier for everyone around him. The differences between the two of them were the first sign that Grant needed extra help.

This dynamic continued throughout their childhoods. When they went to preschool, Bryce had no trouble adjusting. He made friends right away, and seemed to enjoy the daily structure and routine. Grant, on the other hand, always reacted badly to authority. He had trouble playing with the other kids and following rules, and it was no surprise to me when my first conference with his kindergarten teacher started with the words "I'm very concerned about Grant."

The years that followed were tumultuous in every possible way. As I shuttled Grant from one expert to the next, receiving multiple conflicting diagnoses, my husband, John, and I decided to divorce. He is a wonderful father and a good, kind man, but he and I were simply not a good match for each other. Though we were determined to keep our split amicable for the boys' sake, this unfortunately didn't always seem possible. We fought over everything from custody of the boys to the house to the proper diagnosis and treatment for Grant.

I tried my hardest to shield the boys from these arguments, but I constantly worried that the conflict was having an impact on them. Maybe I was making the wrong decision by getting a divorce. Perhaps I should have just stayed with their dad for their sakes. When I wasn't worrying about Grant, who was really putting me through the wringer with his bad behavior, these doubts often kept me up at night.

Of course, there were plenty of good times, too. Grant remained a loyal and proud big brother. He and Bryce were very different, but they connected over their mutual love of nature. We spent many of our weekends at Joshua Tree National Park, and I loved watching Grant teach Bryce about plants and animals as they dug in the ground and explored.

We eventually settled on a diagnosis of bipolar disorder for Grant and stabilized him through a combination of medication, supplements, and nutrition, but we still couldn't seem to find the right school for him. His outbursts and issues with authority kept getting him expelled. Even worse, he had no friends and took all of his anger and frustration out on Bryce, who responded by locking himself in his room and shutting the rest of us out.

I felt constantly torn in two. When I was at work, I was worrying about the boys and feeling guilty for being away from them. When I was with the boys, I was stressing out about money and feeling guilty for not pushing harder in my career. At the end of the day, I was just feeling guilty, period.

After spending many years working as a trainer and nutritionist, I began developing nutrition protocols with doctors. These protocols not only helped countless patients but also helped Grant. Through food intolerance testing that I conducted in the doctors' offices, I found that seven foods were often the culprits behind a wide variety of symptoms, including weight gain and mood swings.

Removing these reactive foods from Grant's diet helped improve his condition even more. Specific foods had a more obvious impact on Grant's brain than on those of other kids. Whenever he ate one of the wrong foods, especially sugar, an outburst would soon follow. I saw it as a gift that his body was talking to me through his mood swings, and I knew that this information could be life-changing for many people.

Our divorce was at last final, and the lawyers' fees had left me nearly bankrupt when I met a literary agent who had the idea to sell my book about food intolerance. She shared my vision, and when a publisher bought that book, *The Virgin Diet,* I knew this was my one chance to get the word out in a big way. I spent my entire advance and then some to create a public television special and hire an amazing business coach who I knew could help me turn the book into a bestseller, ultimately going into an enormous amount of debt to plan a huge launch for the book. No matter what, I wasn't going to lose this chance.

Even better, Grant was in the best state he'd been in his life. His early teen years were so rocky that we ended up sending him to a residential treatment center in Utah for a year, where he worked on his social skills and learned how to manage his explosive behavior. He came back right before his junior year of high school calmer and more self-sufficient than I'd ever seen him.

For the first time, Grant had his own friends to spend time with instead of just hanging around with Bryce and his group of friends. Grant even had his first girlfriend, a sweet girl named Mackenzie, whom he clearly adored.

To everyone's surprise (especially my own), John and I were getting along better than we had in many years and were slowly becoming friends. Since I was traveling so much for work, John moved back into the house to help out with the boys, and I was happy to finally be able to provide them with some stability.

Of course, things weren't perfect. Grant was still hypersensitive and had outbursts from time to time. John and I still argued. But the one area where I really felt I was failing was in my ability to be fully present for the boys. Every day I wrote in my journal, "I need to be more present for my kids." It was the one goal I hadn't made any progress toward. When I was working, I couldn't focus because I was thinking about the boys. When I was with the boys, I was consumed by thoughts of work.

While I made sure to show up for my kids physically, I wasn't always there mentally. I'd spend their entire soccer games and martial arts classes sending emails from my phone. When Bryce came up to me at the end of a game, I had to quickly read the expression on his face to figure out who'd won.

After Grant started dating Mackenzie, he came into my home office to excitedly tell me all about her. As he was talking, I was distracted by something on my computer. One of my staff members had shipped a case of the wrong supplement to a customer. It wasn't until after I had rerouted the shipment and sent out a replacement that I realized I had completely tuned Grant out. He stormed off in anger. The sound of his door slamming shut made me wince.

And there it was in my journal each morning: "Be more present for my kids." For the first time in my life, I did nothing to move forward toward a goal. I knew I needed to do something about it, but I let it slide until it reached the breaking point, as if I were waiting for something to come along and force me to take action.

And then, of course, something did.

Grant had just started his junior year of high school. It was only the second week of school, and he had come home early, claiming that he had a migraine. My rule for the kids was that if they weren't feeling well enough to be at school, then they weren't well enough to go out that day. No fun after-school activities or social plans. But that night Grant said he was feeling better and wanted to go to his martial arts class.

I was still at work when this happened, but John was at home and told Grant that he couldn't go to martial arts. Of course Grant got upset, and with Grant, there's no such thing as a little upset. He begged and pleaded, and when John stayed firm, Grant exploded.

When I got home, John left to go teach a tennis lesson, and Grant immediately turned all his fury on me. "Why are you doing this to me?" he shouted. I was exhausted from a long day at work and knew better than to engage with Grant when he was in this state, so I did my best to stay very calm.

"If your father says you can't go, then you can't go," I told him. John and I had gotten pretty good at co-parenting, especially when it came to our backing up each other's decisions. But no matter how calm or firm I remained, Grant grew angrier and angrier.

"It's not fair!" he screamed at the top of his lungs. "NOT FAIR!"

"Grant, it's okay," I told him calmly. "You'll go to martial arts next time." But nothing would appease him.

"You don't understand," he told me. "I'm not as strong as you think I am." With that, he turned around and walked right out of the house in his bare feet, slamming the door behind him. I took a deep breath to calm myself. No matter how many of these scenes we'd played out over the years, I never really got used to it. They left me with frayed nerves and doubting myself every time.

Maybe I should go after him, I thought. He really was upset. But how many times had I gone after him in similar situations, and what good had it ever done? Maybe the best thing was to let him blow off steam. He was barefoot and didn't have his phone or his wallet with him, so I knew he couldn't go too far, probably just to a friend's house a few blocks away. He finally had friends. I decided to let him be a typical teenager for once and go complain to his friends about his bitchy mom.

I went into the garage and turned my StairMaster on as fast as it would go, needing to blow off some steam of my own. After a few minutes, Bryce came in. As usual, he'd been hiding in his room throughout the whole ugly episode. He looked at me with his good-natured smile. "What a jerk," he said, and although he was smiling, I could tell there was some pain behind his words. My heart ached for both of my sons. It wasn't fair that Bryce had been dealing with this his whole life, but I wished he could see that Grant was just as much of a victim of his brain chemistry as the rest of us were.

John came home from his tennis lesson soon after, and he and Bryce headed out to the store. I figured Grant would be home any minute and things would go back to normal, or at least our family's version of normal. But John and Bryce didn't get more than a few blocks from home before they saw a huge commotion in the road up ahead. Multiple emergency vehicles and police cars blocked the road, their lights flashing a warning. John pulled his car over as close as he could and lowered his window as a policeman approached.

"Was it a multicar accident?" John asked, but the policeman shook his head.

"No, a pedestrian got hit," he said. "We already airlifted him."

John looked at the blood in the road where the body had been. There were no skid marks. Whoever had been hit had been hit hard. "My son was out walking near here," John said slowly.

"Describe him," the cop replied.

John took a breath. "About six feet, two hundred pounds," he began, but the cop interrupted him. The sun was setting by then, and he shined his flashlight into the car to get a better look at Bryce.

"And looks just like him," the cop said matter-of-factly, pointing to Bryce in the passenger seat.

"Grant got hit by a car," John said as he and Bryce stormed into the house moments later. "We need to go to the hospital right now."

I immediately went numb. I felt the urgency, but the full weight of John's words didn't sink in. Without a thought, I grabbed my keys, my phone, and my bag with my laptop and work papers in it and walked out the door. Bryce got into the backseat, and I drove to Desert Regional Medical Center in Palm Springs while John immediately got on the phone from the seat next to me. His first call was to the hospital.

"My son was hit by a car and was airlifted to you," he said. I couldn't bear not hearing what they were saying on the other end, but it turned out they couldn't tell him anything over the phone. I tried to stop myself from wondering if that meant the worst possible news. When I heard the word "airlift," I knew it was serious, but none of this felt real to me yet.

"Call your brother," I said. John comes from a long line of doctors. His brother Herbert is an immunologist, and Herbert's wife, Joan, is the head of Washington University Hospital's Neonatal Intensive Care Unit. They both got on the line with John and told him what we could expect and what to look for when we got to the hospital. The road Grant had been walking on had a speed limit of forty miles per hour, so we knew that if he was still alive, we'd most likely be dealing with a traumatic brain injury.

When we got to the emergency room, I expected them to usher us in to see Grant right away, but instead we had to wait, just like everyone else. I sat down with Bryce in the waiting room as John went to talk to the nurses, but no one would tell him anything. We didn't know if Grant was dead or alive.

I watched the nurses carefully as they spoke to John. Their expressions were blank, but looking closely, I thought I could detect an ounce of pity in their eyes, as if they were thinking, *I sure am glad that I'm not you.*

"It's going to be okay," Bryce said from the seat next to me. I looked down and saw that he was holding my hand. It was surreal to have my fifteen-year-old son console me. "A normal person wouldn't survive something like this," he said, "but Grant's not normal." A small laugh escaped from my lips as I wiped the tears off my face.

Finally, a gray-haired doctor with concerned eyes came out and introduced himself to us as the head of trauma in the emergency room that night. He ushered the three of us into a small conference room. Once we were inside, I immediately panicked. This was not where I wanted to be.

"What was Grant doing out on the road tonight?" the doctor asked me. I just stared at him in silence, not fully understanding the question.

"He was going to a friend's house," John answered for me.

"At what time did he leave the house?" the doctor continued.

"I'm sorry, but why are you asking us these questions?" I finally said. It felt like the doctor was somehow trying to blame John and me for what had happened. "We need to know what's going on with our son."

The doctor nodded and looked at me with practiced sympathy in his eyes. "Grant's injuries are very grave," he said, and then he began ticking them off one by one. "Fractures in both femurs, in his right tibia and fibula. Crushed heel. Distal radius fracture. Floating knee. Right elbow fracture and humeral head fracture."

None of this meant anything to me. What were a few broken bones in the grand scheme of things? "But the worst of it is a skull fracture, a brain hemorrhage, and a torn aorta," the doctor continued. "The neurosurgeon is working to insert a cranial drain now, but the torn aorta kills 90 percent of victims at the scene. The majority of the other 10 percent will die on their way to the hospital."

The doctor paused and turned to John, as if he couldn't bear to say this last part to me. "The chances of him making it through the night are very slim."

"Let me see the scans," John said brusquely, ignoring everything the doctor had just said. John dialed his brother again and read the scans to him over the phone as I stood there, slowly taking in everything the doctor had just told us.

"So what can we do?" I asked the doctor. "There must be something we can do."

The doctor shook his head and spoke quietly. "To save his heart, we'd have to insert a stent," he said. "There are three layers to the aorta, and the inner two have been cut. The outer layer is filling up with blood every time his heart beats," he explained. "His body can't sustain this for much longer."

"Then let's put in the stent," I said.

"Unfortunately, that's not an option in this case," the doctor answered. "We'd have to open his chest to place the stent, and that would require the use of heparin, a blood thinner." He gestured to the scans still in John's hand. "Because of the injuries to Grant's skull, the heparin would cause his brain to bleed out. We can save his brain or we can save his heart, but we can't save both," he summarized.

Just then, John hung up his phone. "Herbert says there are some doctors out there who can do the surgery without a blood thinner," he said. "We just have to find one who's willing to take Grant's case."

The doctor smiled kindly at him. "Your son wouldn't survive the airlift to another hospital, I'm afraid," he told us, "and even if he did, the chance he would survive the surgery is slim, and he would

be so brain-damaged that it wouldn't be worth it." We were all silent for a moment before he continued: "Unfortunately, I think you
have no choice but to let him go."

I knew that time was of the essence (to put it mildly), but I
couldn't stand in that stuffy conference room for one more second
with that doctor who seemed to have written my son off as dead
from the moment he arrived at the hospital that night. I stormed
outside and breathed in the warm California night air.

"Let him go," I muttered to myself out loud as I forced myself to
breathe in and out. "Let him go."

What are we doing? I wondered. Maybe the doctor was right.
We were spinning our wheels trying to find a solution when maybe
there wasn't a solution. Maybe my son got hit by a car and died,
and that's where this ended. Who was I to try to fix something the
doctors said couldn't be fixed? And what if they were right? What
if we saved Grant's life but he never recovered, and ended up being
sentenced to a miserable life? That would probably be the most selfish thing I could do. Was that even what Grant would have wanted?

The thing that scared me more than anything was the idea that
I didn't know who I was trying to save. It was pretty clear to me
already that even if he lived, Grant would never be the same. If
a miracle happened and Grant lived, would I be saving a person
who would live a productive and happy life, a depressed young man
in a wheelchair, or a stranger who would wind up severely brain-
damaged and unresponsive?

I tried to clear my mind and focus on the goal I'd been failing
at for so long—to be fully present for my kids. As all my fears and

doubts rose to the surface, I let them pass by unheeded as I focused on my surroundings and just listened. I heard the ebb and flow of sirens as a steady stream of ambulances pulled up to the emergency room entrance. I smelled the mixture of exhaust and pollen from a nearby bed of flowering plants. As I breathed in that scent, I felt the dryness of the Southern California air entering my nose and filling my lungs.

As I focused on these sensations, it suddenly hit me, as clear as anything I had known before or since. I had to fight for him. I had to rise to the challenge and do whatever it would take to save my son. There was no way I would give up on Grant, no possibility of letting him go. I could waste time wishing the situation I was facing was easier, or I could step up and face the challenge. The choice was obvious. It didn't seem like a choice at all.

It might sound crazy, but the divine light of clarity that surrounded me in that moment felt incredibly peaceful. Despite everything that was happening around me, I smiled to myself, feeling relieved and happy to be standing purely in that moment. For the first time in a long time, I was fully tuned into myself and knew exactly what I needed to do next.

With the confidence that I would never be too distracted for my kids ever again, I headed back into the hospital, ready to face whatever was waiting for me there. Grant needed me; I was really here now, and there was no turning back.

ARE YOU A WARRIOR MOM?

Find out at www.WarriorMomBook.com/quiz.

2

We'll Take Those Odds

I marched back into the conference room, determined to convince the doctors that they had to fight for my son's life. When I got there, people were streaming in and out of the room while Bryce and John made phone calls. "What's going on?" I whispered to John. He held up one finger, telling me to wait.

John hung up his phone a moment later. "We found someone who's willing to perform the surgery without the blood thinner," he told me, "but it means airlifting Grant to Harbor-UCLA."

That was a significant move. Los Angeles is a three-hour drive from Palm Desert, California. I looked at the doctor, who was shaking his head yet again.

"I can't recommend moving Grant in his fragile state," he warned us. "The chances of him dying en route are at least 80 percent."

"But what happens if we keep him here?" I asked, flummoxed by the lack of options he was presenting.

The doctor looked at his shoes. "He will most likely die some-time tonight," he said, "but if he survives the night, his chances of dying will increase by 25 percent each day."

"So he dies here or he dies on the way," I said angrily. "What's the difference?" No one answered. I had a feeling the only difference was a lot of work and effort on the part of the doctors to get Grant ready to be airlifted, and the idea that they wanted to save them-selves the trouble was maddening.

"Let me ask you this," John said to the doctor. "What would you do if this was your son?"

All the activity in the room seemed to grind to a halt as the doc-tor silently considered John's question. It was as if he didn't want to give the answer.

"I would airlift him," he finally answered. I breathed in sharply. "But," he continued before any of us could speak, "you have to understand the risk you're about to take. Like I said, 80 percent of patients in his state will die on the way. Of the 20 percent who survive the airlift, only 10 percent will survive the surgery. Of those who survive the surgery, only 10 percent will ever wake up from the coma, and of those who do wake up from the coma, only 10 percent will have any significant brain function ever again."

The picture he was painting was grim enough to make me doubt myself all over again. Maybe it wasn't worth it after all. But then I heard the voice of my brilliant, brave son. "It sounds like you're saying he has about a .02 percent chance of surviving," Bryce said.

"I'm afraid that's right, son," the doctor answered somberly, patting Bryce on the shoulder.

Bryce responded by looking the doctor right in the eye. "We'll take those odds," he told him, and just like that, the decision was made.

Everyone in the room launched into action except for the head trauma doctor, who stood there as if he was refusing to accept our decision. "We're overruling you," I told him plainly. "Why are you still here? Doesn't every minute matter?" The doctor gathered his scans and other papers as if he'd been stung and wordlessly left the room. I knew I sounded harsh, but it was clear to all of us that his job here was done.

As we waited for the hospital to prepare the helicopter that would airlift Grant to Harbor-UCLA, we were able to see him for the first time. Because he had so many open wounds, the risk of infection was high. John, Bryce, and I scrubbed up, put on masks and gloves, and silently entered the triage unit, where a large team of doctors was working on Grant. They had placed an external ventricular drain through his skull to regulate the pressure in his brain and were working feverishly to raise his blood pressure, which had dropped to a dangerously low 60/40 mm Hg.

The only way I can describe what Grant looked like lying on the hospital bed is that his body was broken. There were tubes coming out of his skull, his nose, and his mouth, and his head was so swollen that he was completely unrecognizable. His head had been shaved so the surgeons could insert the drain in his brain. Grant's shaggy hair, which I had begged him to cut just days before, was gone, and I suddenly wanted it back more than anything.

Blood was everywhere, and the bones in Grant's legs were literally sticking out of his skin. Bandages covered a good portion of him, but I could still see that his entire body was covered in road rash. From head to toe, tiny pieces of gravel were embedded in his skin.

It looked as if he were already dead.

The room immediately started to swim around me. I gripped the rail of the bed to avoid passing out. I wanted to be strong, but dealing with blood and guts has never been my strong suit. As I closed my eyes, I pictured Grant as a young toddler just learning how to walk. He had fallen and hit his mouth on a chair and was bleeding. Seeing the red blood spurting from my baby son's perfect mouth, I panicked. Luckily John stepped in and cleaned up the blood, and within moments Grant was fine. I opened my eyes and looked at him now. What wouldn't I have given for something as easy to fix as a split lip.

It was Bryce who spoke first. "Dude," he said to Grant in a completely normal voice, snapping me back into the moment, "you look a little uglier than usual, but if anyone can make it through this, it's you."

I don't think I've ever been more proud of Bryce than I was in that moment. John and I told Grant that we loved him, and then we all walked out of the room. I wrapped Bryce in my arms and cried. Now that the decisions had been made, my emotions finally surfaced, and I let them all out as I sobbed against my son's chest.

As Bryce held me, I was aware that I should have been consoling him, but instead he was consoling me. I knew I needed to take care of him, but in that moment I couldn't, and he stepped right up and took care of John and me. As I was crying, the neurosurgeon who had placed the drain in Grant's skull approached us and pulled down his mask. He was young, and in his scrubs he looked barely any older than Grant.

"He has some brain activity," the surgeon told me quickly. "Good luck." I watched him walk back toward Grant, feeling tremendously grateful. He was the first person to have given us any good news, and at that moment we needed every shred of hope we could get.

The helicopter that would airlift Grant had a strict weight limit, and he alone weighed two hundred pounds. None of us could ride with him. It would be another hour or two before they were ready to airlift Grant, so John, Bryce, and I quickly drove home to gather a few things before driving to meet Grant at UCLA.

It was hard to plan our next steps, because we had no idea what was going to happen. We didn't say it out loud, but we all knew there was a very good chance that we were getting ready to drive three hours to pick up Grant's body. It was also possible that he would survive the surgery but remain in a coma indefinitely.

John and I each packed a few essentials and quickly decided to drive separately so we'd have two cars available for whatever came next. Bryce decided it would be best for him to stay behind at home. He so wisely knew what he needed, and that was the quiet of home and the comfort of his regular routine—or at least some semblance of it. I quickly called a few neighbors and asked them to check in on Bryce while we were gone. Then I gave Bryce one more hug and got in my car, terrified of where I was headed.

● ● ●

Years before, when I was pregnant with Grant, I looked at John before I ever took a pregnancy test or it was confirmed by a doctor and said, "I am pregnant, and it's a boy." That's the type of spiritual connection that Grant and I have always shared. As an adopted kid, I always longed for that special genetic bond, and with Grant, I finally got it. No matter how far we were from each other physically, I could always feel his energy.

As I drove along the freeway toward Harbor-UCLA, I tried to quiet the doubts and fears in my head and focus on my connection to Grant. But for the first time in his life, I couldn't feel him. That lack of connection and the empty feeling it left me with were too much for me to take. If I couldn't feel him, maybe that meant he was already gone.

I decided the best way to keep myself sane was to reach out to friends while I was on the road and tell them what was going on. It was already almost two a.m. on the West Coast, so I called a few friends who I thought might still be up and then a few on the East Coast as it got later and later. All the way to Los Angeles, I talked to friends who were shocked to hear about what had happened and were happy to keep me company while I drove. Alone in the car, I could voice my greatest fears to their disembodied voices.

"I don't think I can feel him," I told the first person I called. "What does it mean that I can't feel him?"

That wise friend found a way to keep me calm. "You're too close to the situation," he told me. "That's why you can't feel him. You need to trust my intuition instead, and I believe Grant is going to make it. It may be a long haul ahead," he warned me, "but he's going to make it."

I began to gain hope, and was able to focus on the positive with the next friend I called. "At least he didn't miss out on everything," I told her. "He had a girlfriend. He was in love. That's something, right?"

By the time I got to the hospital, it was almost five in the morning. I met up with John in the parking lot, and we walked into the emergency waiting room together. Harbor-UCLA Medical Center is a teaching hospital in Torrance, California. Though much of Torrance is a wealthy beach community, Harbor-UCLA is the Level I Trauma Center for the entire South Bay area. That means the emergency room waiting area, which is open all night, becomes a de facto shelter for a huge percentage of Los Angeles' significant homeless population. This emergency room is also where people go who've been shot or stabbed or who've overdosed on drugs.

I knew it was a grim place, but I was wholly unprepared for the reality of the sights and smells in there. I walked into the emergency room and had to walk right out because I almost threw up from the stench. The waiting area smelled like a bathroom that hadn't been cleaned in years. Homeless people covered in feces or urine took up all the seats. There were others standing around bleeding from their wounds. Clutching my stomach, I stepped outside to get some fresh air while John approached the desk.

"My son was airlifted here," I heard John say to the nurses. He came outside to grab me only seconds later. We were ushered into a large, curtained-off room where a team of a dozen or so doctors and nurses was busily working on Grant. He had survived the airlift. I couldn't believe it. There was a big part of me that was sure John had been bringing me inside to identify Grant's body.

I watched the doctors working on Grant in awe. There was a trauma team, a neurosurgery team, an orthopedic team, and a vascular team. They all moved around him seamlessly, like dancers in a perfectly choreographed ballet. I could tell that they were all totally focused on doing whatever they could for Grant. They had their game faces on.

This was an entirely different scenario than at the first hospital, where everyone except that one young neurosurgeon seemed intent on finding a reason to give up. These doctors saw and dealt with horrible things every day, and they were used to giving desperate situations every ounce of hope and energy they possessed.

"Are you the mother?" An older doctor approached me with a warm smile and a confident look in his eyes. I nodded. "I'm Dr. Carlos Donayre," he said, shaking my hand and then John's. "I'm going to be performing the surgery on Grant's heart. Listen . . ." he continued, looking me right in the eye, "I've got this. I do these procedures all the time. This is the sixth one I've done this month."

This was, obviously, the absolute best thing I could have heard in that moment. John and I went back to the waiting room filled with hope. It was scary in there, and the smell was insufferable, but Dr. Donayre's words could have gotten me through anything.

It was almost eight a.m. when Dr. Donayre came into the waiting room and put his hand on my shoulder. "Everything went perfectly. His aorta is now in great shape," he said with a smile.

"You are amazing," I told him, in complete awe.

"No, I'm just a plumber," he responded kindly. "His aorta is now fixed, but I have no idea about his brain. You'll have to ask the neurosurgeon about that."

Dr. Donayre ushered us to the intensive care unit, where Grant was lying on a bed in the corner. I didn't think any room in that hospital could have been scarier than the waiting room, but I was wrong. The ICU was like the set of a horror movie. Patients were handcuffed to their hospital beds screaming out in pain while police officers watched over them dispassionately.

John and I quickly put on scrubs, masks, and gloves and rushed over to Grant. He looked only marginally better than the last time we'd seen him, but in my eyes he looked wonderful. I gingerly held his hand, which was the only accessible part of him. "I love you so much," I told him. "We all love you."

John stepped up and began running his thumbnail up the arch of Grant's foot. His toes curled in response. "That's a good sign," John told me, and then he leaned in to speak directly to Grant. "You have my permission to prove every one of those doctors wrong," he said in a loud, clear voice. "They don't know you like we do."

As if on cue, the orthopedic surgeon approached Grant's bed and asked to speak to John and me. We followed him into a conference room, where the rest of the orthopedic team was waiting for us. I've learned that the conference room is where they take families to give them bad news.

First the doctors presented us with slides of Grant's various fractures. His broken femurs presented the biggest issue, because the bones had sliced right through his skin and threatened his femoral arteries. If they were broached, Grant would simply bleed out. The orthopedic doctors told us their plan to operate on Grant's legs that afternoon.

"We'll do our best," the head surgeon told us, "but we can have him in surgery for only a short amount of time. We can't risk further damage to his brain if his blood pressure drops again."

John and I both nodded our understanding, and the doctors asked us to wait there for the neurologists to come in. Though Grant's situation was still dire, I was feeling pretty good. He'd already survived the airlift and the heart surgery, both of which the doctors had said were unlikely. Maybe John was right, and Grant would continue to prove them wrong.

But when the neurologists came in, they seemed determined to stamp out my hope. They told us that Grant had never regained consciousness after the car had hit him. "He's sedated now," one doctor said, "but earlier he was in a very deep coma." He went on to give Grant the lowest possible score on each of the many different scales they use to measure the extent of a patient's brain injury, including the Glasgow Coma Scale and the Rancho Los Amigos Traumatic Brain Injury Scale.

"His brain has been gravely injured and is suffering multiple bleeds," he told us. "We're doing everything we can to stabilize him, but he'll likely remain in a coma once we do." He paused for a moment, as if he wanted to make sure we understood him. "There's very little chance that he'll ever wake up."

His words felt like a slap across the face. This was exactly what

I'd feared—that we'd go to these great lengths to save Grant, and he'd remain unconscious forever. I rushed back to his bedside, determined to find a sign that this would not prove to be true.

"Grant," I said to him, holding on to his hand through my latex gloves, "we love you so much." I watched him intently, trying to connect to him like I did when he was inside me. But there was nothing. "I love you, and your dad loves you." Nothing.

For the first time that morning, I allowed myself to study him closely from head to toe. He was shirtless, which the doctors had explained was because his brain wasn't doing a good job of regulating his body temperature. His skin, where it was uninjured, was hot to the touch.

It was jarring to see my son's strong, muscular torso contrasted against the half dozen or so machines that were connected to him. When was the last time he had allowed my eyes to linger on his body? I marveled at his manly form. He was so grown-up. When had that happened? It seemed like yesterday that he was just a little boy. Then one of the machines beeped loudly, lighting up. I didn't know which machine was which. All I knew was that every alarm and artificial compression was keeping my son alive.

One by one, I looked at the various tubes: the one in Grant's nose, bringing oxygen to his lungs; the tubes in his brain, managing its pressure and swelling; the IV in his arm, delivering medication; and the tube in his mouth, providing nourishment to his body. Was it possible that Grant's systems would ever take over and function on their own again?

I didn't allow those thoughts to linger. As long as he was alive, there was hope. Grant may not have felt strong on the night of the accident, but I knew how strong he really was, and I held on to the hope that he would defeat the odds and make it through.

My eyes traveled down to Grant's legs, which looked particularly gruesome with the bones sticking out of his torn flesh. There were tiny fragments of glass embedded everywhere in his skin. But his face was, for the most part, miraculously unscathed. I forced my eyes to return there. With his swollen cheeks and no shaggy mop of hair, he looked just like he did as a baby.

I closed my eyes and tried one more time. "Mackenzie loves you." And then I felt it—the slightest squeeze of my hand. I opened my eyes and saw that the muscles in Grant's hand had contracted and were lifting ever so slightly off the hospital bed. I couldn't believe it. He was squeezing my hand.

I knew it could have been just a coincidence, so I decided to test it. "Allison loves you," I said, using a name that I knew held no special meaning for him. Nothing. Grant's muscles relaxed and his hand lay limp in mine. "Bryce loves you." There was a squeeze again. I was sure of it this time.

I jumped out of my chair, still holding on to Grant's hand, and leaned over so I was speaking very close to his face. "You're in there," I told him. "Grant, you're in there. I can feel you."

I dared to reach out and touch his cheek, which was horribly swollen but one of the few pieces of his skin that remained intact. "Flutter your eyes," I told him, and even though they remained closed, I could see his eyes slowly moving underneath his lids. He was trying. He could hear me.

"Grant, I need you to know that we've got this," I told him. "Your name means warrior, and that's exactly what you are." The outer edges of his lips turned up ever so slightly, as if he was trying to smile.

The handcuffed patients around us were still moaning and screaming out in pain, and I wanted to do a dance around that hospital bed. I wasn't having any of what the doctors had said. They couldn't feel Grant's energy the way I did. They had no idea what he was capable of.

NEED EXTRA INSPIRATION IN YOUR WARRIOR MOM JOURNEY?

Watch my documentary for free at www.WarriorMomBook.com/movie.

3

I Don't Need Your Pity,
I Need Your Strength

That afternoon, as I watched Grant being wheeled into surgery to set his broken femurs and place metal rods in them, a single thought entered my mind: *I can't do this alone.* I hated asking for help, but with Grant's life on the line, I was willing to do anything. I didn't know yet exactly what I was facing, but I knew without a doubt that this was not the time to be proud or independent. In order to face whatever came next, I needed more strength than I possessed. I needed help.

Back in the waiting room while Grant was in surgery, I wrote a message to all my friends and family members about what had happened. After summarizing the details of the accident, the heart surgery, and his current medical state, I wrote:

We are at the top trauma hospital. Their game plan is to stabilize him, normalize him, and then they said it is up to him to heal, and it just takes time. I believe differently. I think that with massive prayer, massive healing energy, lots of touch and love, and then the latest cutting-edge info, he has a far better chance, and I am looking for it. Anything you have, please let me know. I fully intend to have this be my son's second chance and to be better because of it. I won't settle for less, and I certainly will not believe for one minute that he might never wake up.

I love you all. I appreciate you so much. Your phone calls, texts, and emails pulled me through the night and some seriously dark despair. Your positivity and light is keeping us all going here, and I know Grant feels it. I have told him about it.

Thank you. Please pray for my son. I don't need your pity, but I need your strength.

In total gratitude,

JJ

I hit send and sat back in my chair. I don't think I exhaled once in the time it took me to write the message. My phone started beeping almost immediately with texts and emails from people who'd received my message. I knew how lucky I was to have such a supportive and well-informed network, but there was another resource I hadn't yet tapped into.

I had thousands of followers on social media that might have been able to help, even if it was just with a positive thought or a prayer, but I was extremely hesitant to share Grant's story so publicly. I had always made it a priority to guard my sons' privacy, but I believed that at this moment the healing power of prayer was more important. I quickly cut and pasted my message and posted it on my public Facebook page before I could question myself any further.

Soon afterward, Grant was wheeled out of surgery. It had been a success. This was wonderful news, because it meant that he was no longer at risk of bleeding out from his femoral arteries. For the moment, at least, his life was out of imminent danger. I knew that he might never wake up, but at least he was alive. As long as he was alive, there was hope.

I spent that night sitting in the chair next to Grant's bed in the ICU, holding his hand and talking to him in between nodding off for a few minutes here and there and worrying. Mostly I watched him, thinking about all the challenges he'd faced in his life so far. It had always been so difficult to watch Bryce thrive in school and socially while Grant constantly struggled to make friends, fit in, and just get along. My greatest wish for him had always been an easier life than the one he seemed destined to live. He was the very last kid something like this should have happened to, setting him back even further.

My phone had continued beeping throughout the night with a continuous stream of calls, emails, and texts from friends and family members responding to the message I'd sent that afternoon. As the sun came up, I stretched my arms above me and circled my neck, trying to rid myself of the kinks that resulted from spending all night in a rigid hospital chair.

I grabbed my phone and scrolled through the messages. Most of them were the typical "Thinking of you!" or "What can I do?" I appreciated them but wouldn't respond until later. There were some about work. The book launch was only a few weeks away. Then my eyes landed on one with the subject "Your son came to me last night." It was from a casual acquaintance of mine named Dorcy, a person I knew was very intuitive and spiritual.

I clicked on the message from Dorcy. "Your son Grant came to see me last night and asked me to tell you that he's going to be fine," it read. "He's worried about you and wants you to take care of yourself."

As I read it, I suddenly felt my connection to Grant stronger than ever, and this filled me with hope and strength. I put the phone down. I had always been pretty skeptical about psychic connections, but Dorcy's message had really gotten to me. As I read it over again, something inside me shifted. I had certainly experienced a visit from the divine last night, and suddenly everything Dorcy said in her message seemed possible.

When I looked at Grant again, I saw a whole different reality. I felt as if I'd been slapped across the face, like Nicolas Cage in *Moonstruck*, and this time I saw the very *best* kid this could have happened to—the one who so badly needed a fresh start.

I had thought all the big decisions had already been made, but Dorcy's message made me realize that I had one more in front of me, possibly the most important one yet. I had to decide whether this was going to be the best thing that had ever happened to Grant and our whole family or the worst. To me, the choice was clear. Once again, it wasn't really a choice. Things would be better this time around. They had to be.

"Grant," I said loudly as I leaned forward, "you are a warrior." I took a deep breath. "You're going to make it through this, and you're going to be better than ever. You're going to come out of this 110 percent."

Grant didn't respond, of course. He was still in a coma and heavily sedated, but I felt more confident than ever that he could hear me. As I looked at him, it seemed to me that he wasn't quite in there. He was off somewhere, but I was sure that wherever he was, he could hear me.

Then and there, I decided that if Grant was going to recover from this to 110 percent, then I could launch the book that I had everything invested in at 110 percent, too. These two outcomes became fused in my mind, and I launched into action, doing everything within my power to make both of them come true.

I turned my attention back to my emails. The ones about work had looked important, and I felt strong enough now to face them. Sure enough, my publishers were in a panic. They already had all the media for the book launch lined up. I was meant to shoot a public television pledge drive and start the book tour in just a few weeks, and they were worried that I wouldn't be able to do any of it with Grant in this state.

I clicked on an email from my agent. "The publishers are kind of freaking out," it read. "Should I talk to them about pushing the pub date?" I clicked reply without hesitation. "No," I typed, leaning forward in my chair. "I'm all in. Let's make this thing huge."

It may sound ridiculous not to push back the publishing date when Grant was lying next to me in a coma, but I knew that would result in a smaller release. Publishers determine when a book will come out months and sometimes even years in advance and plan everything around that date, from the book's placement within the bookstore to arrangements for reviews of the book and radio and TV interviews to support the release. It was too late to change any of those things now, and pushing back the date would mean losing all the marketing and publicity opportunities I'd worked so hard to get. I couldn't let that happen.

There was something else fueling me too. I believed strongly that the information in *The Virgin Diet* could help change people's lives; I had to get the word out. This was nonnegotiable for me, and I was determined to treat it like the life-and-death situation I was facing with Grant.

The first thing that needed to happen for Grant was to move him out of the adult ICU and into the pediatric ICU. He'd been put in the adult ward because he was essentially an adult physically, but it was scary and chaotic in there. Now that he was relatively stable, the pediatric ICU would be a better place for Grant to recover.

In comparison with the adult ICU, the pediatric ICU seemed like heaven on earth. It was quieter and much more peaceful, and Grant looked like André the Giant in the midst of mostly babies and young children. He was a big sixteen-year-old to begin with, and he had swollen up so much from the trauma to his body that he looked huge and truly scary.

Everything had been going well so far, but Grant's medical state was still very fragile. His brain was swelling, creating a dangerous amount of pressure and preventing his brain from getting the oxygen it needed to heal. The doctor on duty when we arrived at the pediatric ICU never left Grant's bedside, closely monitoring the pressure on his brain to make sure it was under control. Just as his shift was about to end, Grant's kidneys, which we knew had been lacerated in the accident, began to falter. That doctor stayed with Grant for twenty-four hours straight, temporarily placing him on dialysis and watching his kidneys closely until he made sure that Grant was finally stable.

John had gone home to be with Bryce and brought him back to the hospital to see Grant. They arrived shortly after Grant's kidneys had stabilized. Now that Grant's condition was stable, the nurses took over the bulk of Grant's care, but the nurses in the pediatric ward were used to dealing with small children. Grant was huge and heavy and needed to be rolled over every few hours to clean his wounds and change his bandages. His body was still covered in road rash, his entire back skinned raw.

When John and Bryce saw the nurses struggling to move Grant, they stepped in without a word, lovingly turning him over and tending to his wounds. Seeing Bryce care for his brother like that took my breath away.

By then I'd been in the hospital for the better part of three days. I took Dorcy's words about taking care of myself seriously, especially with the book launch coming up. First and foremost, I knew I could not get sick—for my own sake as well as Grant's. If I got so much as a cold, I wouldn't be able to visit Grant in the ICU and risk spreading the infection. Grant still had a feeding tube, a central line, and a catheter coming out of his brain—a lot of holes, which meant a lot of opportunities for an infection to enter his body. So outside of his medical state, keeping myself healthy was my number-one priority.

I didn't know if he'd be there for a day or a week or a year. We had to take everything day by day, and I had to find a way to function at a high level and stay focused. To do that, I had to first make sure I got consistent sleep. While John was with Grant, I rented a suite at a Residence Inn that was just a few miles from the hospital so I'd have somewhere to sleep each night. I found a local Whole Foods and bought the biggest cooler I could find. I loaded that cooler up with wild salmon, grass-fed meat, and plenty of organic produce to keep my energy up. Grant's room was up four steep flights, and I found that I could get a pretty decent burst-style workout by running up and down those stairs. Before long, I had established a routine that I didn't have to think about and that allowed me to focus on the only two things that mattered: Grant and the book.

When John was at home, he'd gotten me three pairs of yoga pants, three sweaters, and three workout tops. I woke up at five every morning. I put on my "uniform," made my morning shake, stopped at Starbucks, and got to the hospital by five-thirty. I wanted to be at the hospital when the residents were doing their rounds. Harbor-UCLA is a teaching hospital. Doctors and students were constantly cycling in and out, glancing at Grant's ridiculously thick chart before moving on to the next patient. Someone had to be there for Grant to act as an advocate and ask questions.

After talking to the doctors as they did their rounds, I spent twenty minutes doing burst training on the stairs. I found a gym nearby and made sure to get myself there at least every other day for a quick workout.

I spent the rest of the day talking to Grant as I worked on the book launch from his bedside. The amount of work I had to do for the launch was massive and overwhelming. All I could do was focus on one task at a time. I had gotten over a hundred partners to agree to do mailings, which I had to orchestrate along with book giveaways, bonuses, webinars, and dozens and dozens of interviews for the media. I also had the full-time job of running my company. Prior to Grant's accident, I was already overbooked. I talked to Grant as I worked, quitting at about nine p.m. most nights to drive to the Residence Inn and sleep. John went home during the week to be with Bryce, so it was just me and my routine. I had to make it work.

Friends who visited me in the hospital urged me to take it easy. "Just relax; let's have a pizza," they said, but this was not the time to let down those walls. The only pass I gave myself was that I could have as much coffee as I wanted. I figured I deserved that much! But I knew that I needed massive energy and focus in order to be there for Grant and get the book off the ground, so sleep, exercise, and healthy food were absolutely critical.

In addition to the constant influx of supportive emails, calls, and text messages I received, people started simply showing up at the hospital. One friend sent a healing scroll to hang in Grant's room. Another sent holy water. The item that people sent more than anything else was, oddly, kale. I had friends who drove hours to the hospital with gift baskets from Whole Foods filled with healthy stuff, including kale salad and kale chips. I was 100 percent grateful for every bit of it, but I had to laugh at the amount of kale we were getting. I know this will surprise a lot of people, but I don't really like kale all that much! It's certainly not something that's easy to eat in the hospital. I sent the nurses home every night with shopping bags full of organic kale, happy to spread the wealth.

My friend Dr. Stephen Sinatra asked his energy healer, Tommy Rosa, to call me every morning when I was on my way to the hospital to tell me what was going on with Grant. Even though he never saw Grant himself, Tommy's reports always lined up with what the nurses told me when I arrived. If Tommy said that Grant's temperature was high that morning, I'd show up to find the nurses working to get Grant's temperature down. If he told me that Grant was having a good morning, Grant would squeeze my hand as soon as I grabbed it in mine. This opened my mind even more to possibilities I never would have previously considered.

One gift that arrived at the hospital one day was the book *Proof of Heaven* by the neurosurgeon Eben Alexander. Reading about his near-death experience and journey to meet with the Divine while his body was in a coma filled me with hope. I was desperate for some sort of indication that Grant was going to be okay, and instead I felt that the book gave me proof that even if he didn't make it, there was something else out there for him. I carried that book around every day with me like a prayer book. Every time I looked at it, I told myself, *No matter what, it's going to be okay.*

Some of the gestures that meant the most to me were the ones that came from complete strangers. One family I had never met before drove three hours from the desert to the hospital just to pray at Grant's bedside. I was dumbstruck as I watched them, with their hands joined and heads bowed in prayer, noticing how content they seemed when they shook my hand afterward and thanked me for the opportunity to pray over Grant.

Before long, there were prayer circles happening for Grant all over the world. Christians, Buddhists, Jews, and Muslims were all praying for him, and I was happy to bring them all in. Every religion became my religion. If it wasn't going to hurt Grant, I was willing to try it. When I sat by his bedside, I could feel all of that love and healing energy being directed at him from people around the globe. He was practically glowing.

Of course, there were some people who couldn't hold back their disapproval. When I posted publicly about Grant, one of my followers commented, "Shame on you for doing this on Facebook." I'll admit that one stung. There was one message, though, that still makes my blood boil when I think about it. A woman named Sharon wrote, "You just focus on your sweet son, and your job will be waiting for you when you're done."

I didn't know Sharon, and she sure didn't know me. She didn't know that I was the primary source of financial support for my sons. She didn't know that I'd spent an entire year of my life planning this book launch or that I'd invested over a million dollars in it—a million dollars that I didn't have. If the book failed, I would be facing bankruptcy, and now a pile of medical bills on top of everything else.

Sharon didn't know about the dedicated staff of people who worked for me and relied on me to support their own families, and she certainly didn't know that if I simply stopped working to focus on Grant, not only would my job disappear, but so would the entire company I'd worked so hard to build. And after the investment my publisher had made in me, no one was going to give me another chance. I wouldn't be able to take care of my family. Failure was simply not an option.

So I launched that book from the ICU. "Grant," I said over and over as I typed out yet another blog post and answered interview questions over email, "you are a warrior, and you're going to come out of this better than ever."

The hospital kindly let me use a small empty room to conduct interviews over the phone or via Skype. Most of the time I returned to Grant's bedside after each interview to find things pretty much the same. His eyes were closed, his machines were beeping, and he was unconscious.

As the doctors made their rounds, they tested Grant's neurological system, clapping their hands loudly in front of his face and doing literal titty twisters to try to get a response. It all seemed a bit barbaric—this was not how I would have wanted to wake up from a coma—but if there was a chance it would work, I wasn't going to question it.

Day after day, there was no response, but I was sure Grant could hear me, so I read him every card that arrived at the hospital from friends, teachers, and neighbors, and gently escorted out any doctor who wasn't completely on board with my decision that this would be the best thing that ever happened to us. I didn't want him to hear anything but love and positive messages.

After a few days, the orthopedic surgeon came in to talk to me again about Grant's heel. At that point, I wasn't too concerned about orthopedic issues. Grant had a gaping wound and a screw sticking out of his heel. It was disgusting, and I could tell that the wound wasn't healing as it should, but after surviving a torn aorta, a crushed heel seemed like no big deal. I remembered years earlier when Bryce had broken his leg doing gymnastics and I thought it was the end of the world, and laughed at my own lack of perspective back then.

"The injury to Grant's heel is a game changer," the doctor told me now. "We're doing our best to get him to the point where he'll be able to walk again if he ever wakes up." I quickly ushered the doctor out of Grant's earshot. I didn't want him to hear that not waking up and never walking again were even distant possibilities.

"No," I said once we'd gotten into the hallway, "Grant is an athlete. He's got to do more than walk again."

The doctor sighed. "We're doing what we can," he told me, "but his heel is completely crushed. At this point, I'd say he'd be very lucky to walk out of here one day." He explained that Grant had a comminuted fracture, meaning the bone had shattered into three or more fragments. In addition, the bones had broken through the skin, damaging the surrounding muscles, tendons, and ligaments.

I paused for a moment. I knew it was bad, and I could tell that the doctor was trying to help Grant, but I wanted to make sure that he shared my goals, that he was aiming not just to help Grant live but to thrive. I could tell that his entire course of action would be different if he was looking for the same outcome that I was, and I racked my brain for a way to communicate this to him.

"What would you do for Kobe Bryant?" I asked him finally. "Whatever you would do for him, I want you to do for Grant. Or else I need to get Kobe Bryant's doctor in here."

The doctor smiled. "Okay, Mom," he said, but I could sense that something had changed. He knew that I wasn't going to accept "good enough." Either he could rise to the occasion or we'd find someone who would.

The doctors' negativity wasn't the only thing we worked to shield Grant from. The pediatric ICU was calmer than the adult unit, but some horribly sad things happened there. Later that same day, a girl who had cerebral palsy was brought in. The doctors all knew her, and I quickly ascertained that she'd been in and out of the ICU many times before. The girl was seizing when she got to the hospital, and as the doctors streamed in to work on her, I heard Grant's doctor say, "She's not going to make it this time."

John had brought some of Grant's favorite music from home, so I turned it up as loud as I could, and I threw myself across Grant's broken body in my best effort to shield him. It was obvious that the doctors were doing everything they could for this girl. They were trying to insert a breathing tube but were struggling to treat the seizure and her respiratory compression at the same time. Soon she was coding. The doctors still didn't give up. They kept trying to get the breathing tube in and get a heartbeat back until she took her last breath.

Tears streamed down my face as I held on to Grant, focusing all my energy on keeping him from hearing what was going on around him. I couldn't go back in time and protect him from the car that had hit him, but I was determined to use everything in my power to protect him from this.

TAKING CARE OF YOUR FAMILY MEANS TAKING CARE OF YOURSELF!

Get quick tips to make it easier at www.WarriorMomBook.com/tips.

4

Now We Wait

During the first few weeks after the accident, the story of what had happened that night slowly worked its way to John and me. We learned that a neighbor who was driving down the road had heard the impact of the car hitting Grant and quickly made his way to the scene. No one actually saw the car hit Grant, but the police estimated that it was going about forty miles per hour. That was the speed limit, and there were no skid marks in the road. The driver didn't have time to hit the brake.

As our neighbor approached the scene, he saw a white car pulled over to the side of the road near Grant's body and glass all over the road. A woman got out of the car and surveyed the damage before stopping to look at Grant lying there. From her perspective, he must have looked dead. She didn't wait to find out.

Quickly she got back in her car and sped away as our neighbor called 911.

While John and I were focused on Grant, there was another journey going on simultaneously—the search for this woman, the driver. It was something I paid very little attention to. I had my two priorities—Grant and the book—and had no energy left over to devote to anything else.

My physical and mental presence was needed each moment at the hospital. I had to make life-altering decisions nearly every day. If I'd wasted even one second thinking about the woman who'd caused this, it would come at the expense of my ability to be fully present for Grant. In his state, Grant couldn't afford that, and neither could I.

Not everyone agreed with my approach. Many of our friends and family members were filled with rage toward this woman whom we knew nothing about. There were so many questions, so many unknowns, and a lot of people seemed to think that finding her would somehow give us the answers we so desperately wanted. But the truth was, she didn't know the truth about what would happen to Grant from this point on any better than the rest of us did.

When one of my best friends came to visit for the first time in the hospital, she told me, "I'll put up a reward of ten thousand dollars to go after that woman." I just looked at her. The offer was incredibly generous, but in my mind it was pointless.

"Why?" I asked her. Grant lay beside me motionless. The doctors still claimed that he would never wake up, but I refused to believe them. Either way, I was certain that finding the woman whose car had hit him wouldn't change his outcome one bit.

My friend was shocked by my response. "Don't you want to go after her?" she asked me.

I just shook my head and looked back at Grant. No matter how much we might have wanted to, none of us could change what had happened on the night of the accident. What was done was done. All we had now were the facts in this moment. Grant was in a coma and needed the best possible care that we could get for him. Finding this woman wouldn't help with that.

I smiled at my friend. "I love you," I told her. "Thank you. But if you want to put up that kind of money, put it toward Grant's care. That's what I'm going to focus on, and I appreciate you putting your energy there too."

No matter how many times I repeated those words, plenty of people still persisted in their efforts to find the driver. On one level, I understood this. They wanted a villain to blame for Grant's condition, and it was easy to project all their anger and fear about the situation onto this nameless, faceless woman.

Of course I was angry and afraid too, but I was less certain that the driver deserved all the blame for what had happened to Grant. He had been angry and flustered when he left the house that night. Maybe he wasn't paying attention and had stepped in front of the car. Maybe she was texting. Did any of that even matter?

Yes, the driver absolutely should have stuck around and gotten Grant help, but I didn't know anything about her situation and why she may have been terrified to face the police. And frankly, whatever was going on with her wouldn't have made one ounce of difference to the boy who was currently lying unconscious in a hospital bed.

Besides being a pointless activity, spending time thinking about the driver brought my spirits down. As I focused on Grant and the book, I forced myself to tune out anything and everything that didn't fill me with hope. All my fears and doubts lurked right under the surface, just waiting for someone with the wrong mindset to come along and bring them to light.

My mother wanted me to call her every day with an update, but I knew I couldn't do that. I promised her that I would post an update on Facebook each night and tried my best not to feel guilty about her disappointment. I love my mother dearly, but she operates from a place of fear, and I knew that talking to her every day during this time would send me right down in a fear spiral with her.

I often found myself caught in that spiral anyway, especially on Fridays. They were always the hardest day of the week for me when Grant was in the hospital. It was just so quiet and lonely. The nurses seemed upbeat as they looked forward to their well-deserved weekends, and it was hard to watch them as I wondered when any of us would have anything resembling a normal weekend again. As the doctors and nurses went through their shift change, my own what-if shift started. I watched the staff leave for the weekend, thinking, *What if he doesn't get any better?*

Luckily, I had people around me who wouldn't let me spend too much time indulging in these thoughts. Dr. Anne Meyer, a rehabilitation doctor who works in the brain trauma unit at Cedars-Sinai Medical Center, showed up one Friday night armed with essential oils and a positive outlook. I'm not sure which was more helpful. I barely knew Dr. Meyer before this, but she somehow knew exactly what both Grant and I needed.

Dr. Meyer interrupted the what-if shift that night by matter-of-factly unpacking her essential oils kit and explaining what they were. "These are the life force of a plant and the equivalent to our blood, which carries oxygen," she told me. "The sense of smell is the only one of our senses that is directly connected to our limbic system, which includes the hippocampus and the amygdala. When you breathe in these oils, they directly activate the hypothalamus."

She held a small bottle of lavender oil out for me to sniff. "Do you mind?" she asked, gesturing toward Grant. I nodded immediately. If there was even the slightest chance this could help Grant's brain heal, of course I wanted to try it.

She poured a tiny amount of the oil onto her palms and began to rub it on Grant's temples. "As Grant breathes in the essential oils, they'll go up into his nasal passages and trigger his limbic system," she told me before moving on to his big toes. "In reflexology, the big toes are thought to reflect the brain. The oils will send stimuli throughout the electrochemical pathway to help it heal."

We spent an hour or so chatting as she rubbed various oils on every part of Grant's body that she could access. "Grant is doing great," she told me before she left that night.

"How can you tell?" I was so desperate to hear any good news. The doctors always told us what was going wrong. It was a breath of fresh air to hear something positive.

"Some people who have a brain injury develop spasticity," she said. "It's not a muscle spasm like you or I might get—it's a central nervous system issue, and it's involuntary."

This was the first I'd heard about this condition, and I started to get nervous. Was this one more thing we needed to worry about? "When patients don't have spasticity, their recovery is so much greater," she said. "Grant doesn't have it. Isn't that exciting?"

I had been watching Grant as she spoke. "Yes," I said, feeling relieved. "That is exciting."

Dr. Meyer began packing up her oils. "And look at his blood pressure," she told me, gesturing toward one of the many machines that were still keeping my son alive. "It's gone down since I've been here," she noted. "I'd say the oils are working their magic already."

After she left, I noticed that Grant's nose had begun to twitch ever so slightly, and as I spoke to him, he wiggled his toes. *It really is working,* I told myself as a grateful smile spread across my face. *It's working.*

Of course we still didn't know if Grant would ever wake up or what he would be like if he did. The doctors kept warning me that if and when he came out of the coma, it was going to be "ugly," but I had no clue what that meant. I thought he'd wake up, scream for a minute, and then look me in the eyes and say, "Hi, Mom, I love you." Instead, he just lay there.

"What do we do now?" I asked Grant's head doctor the next day as she did her rounds.

"We wait," she told me kindly.

"We wait?" I couldn't believe there wasn't something more that we could do.

"Yes," she said in a firm voice. "The brain has its own timetable. All we can do is wait."

This contradicted the advice that had been pouring in from my community of health experts. Shortly after we began using the essential oils, one of my girlfriends put me in touch with Dr. Donald Stein, who'd been studying progesterone therapy in the treatment of traumatic brain injuries for decades.

When we spoke on the phone, Dr. Stein explained to me that women had proven to recover better from TBIs because of their higher levels of progesterone. In his studies, injections of progesterone given within forty-eight hours of a brain injury produced dramatically lowered rates of brain swelling and far better neurological outcomes.

Grant was already outside that window, but Dr. Stein said there was a chance it could still help him, so John and I took turns rubbing progesterone cream on him every day. We repeated, "You are a warrior," over and over as we massaged him with the cream.

Another friend sent me an article by Dr. Barry Sears, who in 2006 had consulted on the first-ever case of using high-dose fish oil to treat traumatic brain injuries. The brain of a miner named Randal McCloy Jr. was badly damaged by carbon monoxide after a deadly explosion in West Virginia. McCloy started out in critical condition, and it was expected that he would be severely brain-damaged if he survived, but after receiving high doses of fish oil each day, he made a miraculous recovery and returned home only two weeks later.

I was already familiar with the use of fish oil to treat the brain. In fact, before the accident Grant had been on five grams of fish oil per day as part of the treatment for his bipolar disorder. The cell walls of the brain are composed in part of omega-3 fatty acids, which are found in fish oil. They're the building blocks that the brain needs to heal itself after an injury.

When I spoke to Dr. Sears from the hospital, he explained that when the brain experiences a profound injury, neurons snap, setting off a wave of inflammation in the brain that can smolder for a long time unless there's a second response that turns it off. The omega-3 fatty acids in fish oil, which are naturally anti-inflammatory, can act as that second response.

Dr. Sears pointed me toward medical literature describing seven cases of high-dose fish oil as treatment for traumatic brain injury, including one very similar to Grant's. A teenager named Bobby Ghassemi nearly died as a result of injuries sustained in a car accident. He was treated with a large infusion of fish oil. A few months later, he attended his high school graduation.

Grant still had a feeding tube, so I couldn't give him fish oil myself. The hospital would need to put it in his IV. Feeling hopeful and inspired, I brought the information I'd gathered about fish oil and brain injuries to Grant's doctors, but they immediately shut the idea down. They claimed that high doses of fish oil could cause excessive bleeding and were concerned that Grant would bleed out if the fish oil caused his bleed times to increase.

When I looked at the literature, I couldn't find one study that showed fish oil extended bleeding times. I continued pushing the issue, citing the fact that Grant had already been on fish oil prior to the accident. The doctors finally relented, but they wouldn't give him more than two grams. I was frustrated that Grant wasn't getting the high doses that I was sure he needed, but I tried to focus on the good news that at least he was getting some.

As I sat by Grant's bedside, I couldn't stop myself from going back to the night of the accident and asking myself if our argument about his martial arts class was the last time Grant and I would ever speak. I remembered dropping Grant off at day care when he was a toddler. He would cry hysterically, his face growing red and blotchy as he desperately tried to reach out for me. The caretakers told me that he was always fine just a moment after I left, but our terrible parting left me feeling awful for the rest of the day. This felt just like that, but so much worse.

Over and over, I replayed it in my mind. The argument. The sound of the door slamming shut. The image of Grant storming away in his bare feet. Above the din of the hospital I heard Grant's last words to me: "I'm not as strong as you think I am." What had he meant by that? On the one hand, I knew that it was just his teenage way of trying to manipulate me. He wanted me to think that I was being too hard on him so that I would cave and let him go to martial arts. But my guilt clouded my judgment, making me think that I should have done something—anything—differently to stop what had happened.

This was the what-if spiral that I tried desperately to stay out of, but sometimes I still ended up there. It was like quicksand, sucking me down into its depths if I set so much as a toe in. *What if I'd just let him go to martial arts? What if I'd stopped him from leaving the house? What if I hadn't come home when I did?* There were so many ways the accident could have been avoided, but I couldn't go back and change any of them. The only way out of this spiral was to focus on what I could do now. I couldn't change the past, but I could certainly take steps to change the future, and that idea was incredibly empowering.

So I kept going. I got up at five, talked to Grant as I worked on the book, and ran the stairs. I didn't think about it. I just did it. There were plenty of days when I didn't know where I would get the inspiration to keep moving forward. If I wasn't careful to manage my mindset at every moment, I'd quickly spiral downward. So I kept running up and down those stairs, trying to sweat away all my fears.

What if Grant never wakes up? What if he wakes up but is severely brain-damaged? What if the book is a failure and I lose everything? These questions threatened to take me down on a daily basis, but I just continued going, pushing forward, and doing my best to keep choosing hope.

ARE YOU A WARRIOR MOM?

Find out at www.WarriorMomBook.com/quiz.

5

Let's Go

I remember celebrating many years ago when my boys were finally out of diapers. Because the two of them were only one year apart, it felt as if I'd spent a lifetime buying, changing, and discarding diapers. By the time they were both potty trained, I knew I probably wouldn't have any more kids. As I boxed up all the remaining diapers in our house to give away, I said to John, "Thank God I never have to change another poopy diaper."

Imagine my surprise over a decade later when my teenage son's soiled diaper was a reason to celebrate. Grant's bowel movements were the first sign that he was starting to come out of the coma and begin the long, slow, and sometimes painful process of awakening.

That weekend John was at the hospital and helped the nurses turn Grant over to clean and dress his wounds, and he noticed that the road rash on Grant's back was starting to heal. This told us that his immune system was re-creating cells. The catheter to release the pressure on Grant's brain was still hard at work, but as I sat at Grant's bedside day after day, I saw that there was less and less fluid coming out of the tube. His brain was getting better at absorbing the fluid itself the way a healthy brain does.

As the doctors did their rounds, they constantly monitored what was going on with Grant neurologically. After Grant had been in the coma for two weeks, his eyes were open and both of his pupils were dilated. As part of their routine checks, the doctors shined a light in Grant's eyes to see if his pupils were symmetrical and whether they'd react to the light. They clapped loudly right in front of his face and shouted his name from a few inches away to see if he would respond to the noise. Day after day, he didn't. We didn't know if this meant he was deaf or severely brain-damaged or simply not aware enough to hear it yet. We just had to wait and see.

Now when I spoke about Bryce or Mackenzie, Grant consistently squeezed my hand. The hospital initially wouldn't allow Mackenzie in to visit Grant because she wasn't family. John pled our case to the doctors and hospital administrators, threatening to have Grant transferred to another hospital if they didn't let her in to visit him.

I was so grateful for John in those moments. I had taken on the role of Mama Bear and knew I could be abrasive at times, but John always knew how to smooth things over and get results. Thankfully, the powers that be agreed to let Mackenzie visit, and I appreciated her commitment to traveling back and forth to see Grant. It was a lot to ask of a young girl, but it was clear how important her presence was to Grant.

Perhaps Grant's most meaningful response at this stage was involuntary. Every time Mackenzie or I walked into the room, Grant's blood pressure immediately dropped. Our presence calmed him. He really could feel me and hear me. That knowledge alone was enough to inspire me to keep pushing forward.

The signs that Grant's body was moving closer and closer to consciousness came day by day, minute by minute. Sometimes when I talked to him, his eyelids fluttered. As I had when he was a baby, I made sure to praise him every chance I could. "Good job, Grant," I told him. "You fluttered your eyelids!" A day or two later, he just barely sighed. "Today was a good day," I wrote as part of my nightly Facebook update. "Grant sighed." It struck me how much my definition of a "good day" had changed.

I wouldn't have been able to pinpoint the exact moment when his doctors changed their attitude toward Grant, but once they saw that he was moving in a positive direction, they started treating him—and us—completely differently. I always had hope for a good outcome for Grant, but now the doctors finally did too. The pity was gone from their eyes when they spoke to John and me, and they were suddenly interested in moving things forward. They wanted to remove the catheter from his brain and wean him off the ventilator to see if he could breathe on his own.

I was more concerned about getting his feeding tube out so I could get some real nutrition into him. Now that his swelling was going down, Grant was rapidly losing weight. The feeding tube wasn't providing him with enough nutrition. I knew how important good nutrition was for his brain to heal, and that the measly two grams of fish oil he was getting wasn't going to cut it. Unfortunately, he couldn't swallow for himself yet, so for the moment we had to continue relying on his feeding tube.

When Grant first arrived at the hospital, John and I had asked the doctors not to make any big decisions without at least one of us present. But one day they decided to remove the catheter from his brain with no warning at a rare moment when neither of us was there. Removing the catheter stressed Grant's heart. When I got to the hospital that morning at my regular time, Grant's heart rate was going through the roof. It went up to 210 beats per minute, which I knew his heart wouldn't be able to sustain for long.

It seemed like at any moment the stent in his aorta would fail and his heart would stop. I didn't leave his side for a day and a half until his heart rate started to go down. He was finally stable, but it was impossible to know if any damage had been done to his heart.

Once Grant was stabilized again, the doctors began to slowly wean him off the ventilator. They started by giving him fewer breaths per minute, allowing him to establish his own rhythm. It was terrifying to watch the machine that monitored his blood oxygen level and see it go up and down. I knew how important it was for him to reestablish his own breathing rhythm, but his brain needed as much oxygen as possible to heal and prevent further damage.

For days, Grant's eyes had been fluttering open and closed, and then suddenly they were open. This was a miracle, but yet again, it didn't happen the way I expected it to. Instead of looking directly at me, or at anything, he stared vacantly into space. He was coming back, but he still wasn't really there.

The first thing Grant moved was his left arm, one of the only parts of his body that wasn't covered in a cast or a bandage. So slowly that it was almost painful, Grant began to move his left arm back and forth across his torso. It was a twitchy and disquieting pattern of movement back and forth and back and forth as he stared blankly into space.

This went on for hours and hours, and while I knew on an intellectual level that any movement, any progress, was good, inside I felt crushed. *Is this what the rest of his life will be like?* I wondered as I watched his arm move back and forth again and again and again. Of course I was happy to be able to hold Grant and see him there in front of me, but I still couldn't help but wonder if we'd made a huge mistake by trying to save him.

I was eager to push Grant's progress forward by any means possible, so I tried everything I could think of to get a response from him. I brought in Popsicles and lollipops to test his sense of taste. The first time I put one to his lips, he pursed them just a tiny bit. He could taste it!

Grant's responses grew minutely each day. He went from barely being able to purse his lips when he tasted a Popsicle to licking his lips to taste more. His progress at this stage was so subtle that if I hadn't been completely focused and tuned into him, I might have missed it. When I spoke to him, I often leaned in close to his face. "I love you, Grant," I said, and as I backed away, still watching him, I noticed his eyes just barely track my movement.

"Grant!" I shouted at the top of my lungs, calling for the attention of one of the nurses on duty, and he startled almost imperceptibly at the sound. "He tracked me," I told the nurse as she rushed into the room. She immediately turned on her penlight, and sure enough, Grant tracked it an inch or so from side to side.

Before long, he started to track me farther, and then when I talked to him, he began to look in my general direction. All these positive signs fortified me against the inevitable setbacks. Grant's temperature was still inconsistent, and he often had a fever. This told us that his hypothalamus, which controls the body's temperature, wasn't healed well enough to monitor his body's delicate balance between heat production and heat loss. Grant's heart rate also fluctuated dangerously.

But the hardest part was the fact that we didn't know how long any of this would take. When would he fully wake? When would he talk? Would he be able to walk? There are stages of a coma, but they're not clearly defined because they're so different for each individual. Nobody could tell us what would happen next. When I asked the doctors, all they said was "It's going to be ugly" and "It will take time." Both statements felt as hopeless and repetitive as the movement of Grant's arm.

As Grant's systems unfolded, the doctors kept him somewhat sedated. It was important for him to be able to gain consciousness, but patients coming out of a coma are often volatile. Grant was big and strong, and if he became fully aware, they knew he would likely pull out his tubes, pushing back his progress. It was another delicate balance that I watched closely for any sign of improvement.

Either John or I was at Grant's bedside at every moment, giving him as much input as possible. It was exhausting to keep up a cheerful monologue while my son lay there endlessly moving his arm back and forth across his body, but I felt so strongly that Grant could hear me. I wanted him to know I was there.

Ever since Dorcy had sent the message about Grant worrying about me, I felt that even in this state Grant could sense my moods. This was something he'd always been able to do. So I worked hard to manage my fear and my self-talk. If Grant was going to be feeding off my feelings, I was going to make sure they were healthy ones.

Most days I just barely made it through on a steady diet of adrenaline, coffee, and hope. But by the time I left the hospital at night, I often felt as if I was going to collapse from the stress of the situation. I didn't think I was strong enough to keep going. But what choice was there? I had to stay strong for Grant.

John, Bryce, and I buoyed one another up. Most weekends, John brought Bryce with him to the hospital. Bryce was amazing with Grant, and Grant responded so well to him. I wanted them to be around each other as much as possible. It was also obvious to me that this was all taking a toll on Bryce. He was still doing well in school, but he was having trouble sleeping and suffering from migraines. At least when we were together, we could hold one another up. Bryce was in good spirits when he was with us. It may sound strange, but we managed to share some good moments together huddled around Grant's hospital bed.

"Squeeze my hand," we told Grant. "Wiggle your toes." He began to respond faster and more consistently, so we repeated these instructions to him again and again and again. We had to be careful not to overstimulate him. He would typically respond to the first few commands and then go back to sleep. Then we kept talking to him while he was sleeping until he was ready to try again.

Soon afterward, Grant reached his left arm down to his torso to scratch an itch—an involuntary movement that most of us do a hundred times a day—but this was a huge milestone for Grant. This meant he had felt an itch and was able to make the connection and scratch it. One of the nurses and I cheered and high-fived each other next to Grant's hospital bed. It was clear that Grant was coming back, but we still didn't know the full extent that he would.

Now if I clapped my hands, he'd turn and look at me. He could track the bright lights on the television. One night one of the *Transformers* movies was on the TV. Grant was staring straight ahead at the screen, but we didn't know how much of the movie was getting through to him.

The night nurse came in and suddenly yelled out his name: "GRANT!" He turned his head and looked at her, with his brow knit and an expression of mild irritation on his face, as if she had interrupted him. This was a level of awareness we hadn't seen since the accident. Every small victory was another reason to celebrate.

The only tube Grant had in him now was the feeding tube, which I wanted out so I could get some real nutrition into him. Grant was down to about 145 pounds from his original weight of over 200. "Honey," I said one morning as I stood next to his bed, "we have to get this feeding tube out so we can get you some good food. That will help you heal." All of a sudden, Grant started making a horrible gagging sound, as if he was going to throw up.

"What's happening?" I asked John, who was there for the weekend, in a panic, about to ring for the nurse.

"He's hacking it up," he said, jumping up from his chair. John grabbed the end of the feeding tube. Grant had regurgitated all but the last few inches of it, which John easily pulled out.

For me, this was one of the biggest milestones yet, because it meant I could jump into action in the field that I knew best— nutrition. I went out and got a blender and all sorts of supplements and started feeding Grant superpowered smoothies that were full of l-glutamine and amino acids, probiotic yogurt, and fish oil. I gradually upped the amount of fish oil I gave him, keeping a close eye on his bleed times, which thankfully stayed consistent.

There was no fridge at the hospital for me to use, so I brought a cooler full of food with me every day. Parking near the hospital was always a disaster, so I had to drag everything from a mile or more away to the hospital doors. Grant's doctor shook her head one morning at the sight of me struggling to get everything into the room. "I can't believe you're doing that," she told me. "No other parent has ever done all that."

I looked at her and responded honestly. "Well, I can't believe they don't," I said. The hospital food was horrible, and I knew how important good nutrition was for Grant's brain. Eventually, I had to post a sign on his door reading, "No Ensure, No Crystal Light." I couldn't believe that they wanted to feed artificial sweeteners to a young man with a brain injury.

As I fed Grant, I explained what I was giving him and what it would do, all along telling him that it would make him better than he was before. "Here's some fish oil to heal your brain," I said, and he opened his mouth and swallowed it. "There's so much we can do for you. I've got all the best doctors working to help you get better than ever."

Now he looked right in my eyes as I fed him, and I could tell that he heard me. "This has probiotics," I said, switching over to the yogurt. "It's helping your gut heal. You are a warrior."

Once Grant could chew and swallow, we moved on to solid foods. John went out one weekend and got Grant a huge grass-fed beef burger with mushrooms and barbecue sauce—his favorite. John held it up for Grant to take a bite, and his eyes rolled back in his head as if he were in heaven. Every time he finished chewing and swallowing one bite, he popped his mouth open like a hungry little bird. We were all in a celebratory mood, cheering Grant on as he ate his burger.

The nurses came in one by one and smiled at Grant like proud aunties watching a baby eat his first meal. Whenever John turned away from Grant to say something to one of the nurses or to me, Grant smacked his lips to get John's attention so he would give him another bite. The nurses thought this was hilarious. "Watch out, Dad, he's hungry," one of them warned as she went back to work, smiling from ear to ear.

Soon afterward, Mackenzie came back to visit. I had to leave the hospital to tape the audio recording of *The Virgin Diet*, and John decided to take advantage of having another visitor around so he could take a break. I was in the recording booth when my cell phone rang.

It was Mackenzie. "What's wrong?" I asked as I instantly grabbed the phone.

"Nothing. Grant talked to me," she responded. "He told me he loved me."

I could not believe it. By the time I got back to the hospital, John was already there. Grant looked right in our eyes, and I saw my son. I recognized him, and I knew he could recognize us. He darted his eyes to the tray of hospital food that sat uneaten on a nearby table. "Disgusting," he told us slowly, and I burst into a strange half laugh, half cry.

"That's my boy," I said to John, putting my hand on Grant's cheek.

For days, the only words Grant spoke were "I love you," to me, John, and Mackenzie, and "Home," in an insistent, angry voice. He didn't seem to know where he was or how he'd gotten there, but he wanted to go home.

John and I thought it would be important for Grant both mentally and physically to get into a different position and have a change of scenery. John knew about something called a cardiac wheelchair, which adjusts vertically so that patients can go from lying to sitting without placing a burden on the heart. He insisted that every hospital had one.

When the head nurse came to do her routine vitals check, John asked her, "Do you have a cardiac wheelchair?"

She looked puzzled. "What's that?"

John sighed. "Let me talk to the nurse who's been here the longest," he said, and when she came in, John told her, "Somewhere in this hospital is a cardiac wheelchair."

To my surprise, her eyes lit up with recognition. "You know, I think I know where that is," she said.

During her next break, John went with the nurse, and they found a cardiac wheelchair buried in the back of a supply closet. Together they began the painstaking process of loading Grant into the wheelchair. Since the feeding tube had come out, he'd been steadily gaining weight, but he still couldn't support himself.

As he struggled to lift him, John grunted, "He's like a 150-pound bag of Jell-O." Grant's left leg was still in a cast, and the nurses had to tie it to the leg of the wheelchair for support. The entire process of loading Grant into the wheelchair and getting him outside took over an hour, but the expression on Grant's face once we got out into the fresh air made all that effort more than worth it. He closed his eyes and smiled serenely as we pushed him around and around the parking lot and hospital grounds.

From that day on, Grant's favorite words were "Let's go." As soon as John or I got to the hospital in the morning, he'd say, "Let's go. Let's go," and we'd start preparing him for a trip outside. He still slept for much of the day and was somewhat sedated, but as he became more and more aware, Grant grew increasingly frustrated just lying in the hospital bed.

As we spent hours wheeling him around the parking lot, I realized it was time for a greater change of scenery. Now that Grant was medically stable, he needed intensive therapy to regain his cognitive and motor skills. As a trauma center, Harbor-UCLA didn't offer those services.

For a while we tried doing everything we could for him there.

When Bryce came to visit, he played guitar for Grant and tried to get him to sing along. I bought a dozen balls in various shapes and sizes and played catch with Grant from a chair next to his hospital bed.

One day while I was working on the book launch at Grant's bedside, Bryce decided to try something different. Standing close to the left side of Grant's head, he put his right hand on Grant's left shoulder and said, "Hey, Grant, raise your arm." Grant immediately raised his left arm a couple of inches and then dropped it down. I looked up from my laptop. That was the fastest he'd ever responded to one of our commands.

"Raise your arm," Bryce said again. This time Grant got his arm up maybe four or five inches off the bed. I watched with an amazed smile on my face as this continued for several more minutes. Each time, Grant raised his arm a little bit higher than the last, until he finally got it high enough to reach Bryce's shoulder. As he rested his hand there, Bryce moved his own hand from Grant's shoulder to the top of his head. They stood there, intertwined, just staring at each other as I silently cried. It was the most connected I'd ever seen the two of them.

Grant's language was still mostly limited to "I love you" and "Let's go," but when I brought a deck of cards to play blackjack with him, I could tell he had some level of recall. Every day I showed him pictures of his friends and of Mackenzie, repeating their names to help him remember who they were.

I had been kissing Grant for weeks since the accident with no response, and then one day when we were playing blackjack, he pursed his lips to kiss me back. He looked like a fish with his lips in an exaggerated pucker, but it was by far the best kiss I'd ever gotten.

Each step forward filled me with confidence and hope—and the urge to do more. I wanted to make sure we were helping Grant continue to progress instead of letting him backslide, so I was in a rush to rehabilitate him as quickly as possible. John and I researched local hospitals that offered the type of therapy Grant needed and agreed to transfer him to Children's Hospital Los Angeles as soon as possible. I was eager to get Grant completely off the drugs that were keeping him sedated and get him started on therapy. I had no idea that this would pose a completely new set of obstacles.

NEED EXTRA INSPIRATION IN YOUR WARRIOR MOM JOURNEY?
Watch my documentary for free at www.WarriorMomBook.com/movie.

6

It's Going to Be Ugly

It was early November and still hot in Southern California, and I arrived at the hospital in a great mood, dressed in a tank top and yoga pants. It was finally the day Grant was going to be transferred to Children's Hospital Los Angeles. I had gotten up at sunrise to pack my car full of Grant's things while an ambulance waited by the hospital entrance to transfer him. The night before, I had moved myself from the Residence Inn to a condo I rented in Los Angeles to be closer to the new hospital. I was thrilled to finally be moving forward.

As Grant had gradually become more and more aware, I saw what the doctors had meant when they said, "It's going to be ugly." It was as if there were two Grants—the sweet, smiley Grant who repeated, "I love you, I love you," and the angry, volatile Grant whom John and I referred to as the Incredible Hulk.

The doctors explained that this was normal. When patients with a traumatic brain injury are waking up from a coma, they lack an internal editor. They can be violent, hypersexual, completely devoid of emotion, or anything in between. The doctors and nurses had explained this over and over, but no one could have prepared me for what it would be like to see the TBI manifest itself in my son's personality. He was a different person, and so far, the changes were not for the better. Plus, we still had no idea how long any of this would last.

Grant's primary symptom was agitation. This might have been normal for someone in his condition, but he was big and strong and at times truly scary. When he wanted something, he wanted it now. He was like an overgrown toddler with no patience for his own limitations. He still couldn't walk or say more than a few words, but he desperately wanted to get out of the hospital bed and get moving. Children's Hospital was better equipped to deal with all of Grant's needs, especially his mood swings, and I was eager to get him over there.

Early that morning, I went with Grant as he went to undergo a CAT scan as part of his routine discharge protocol. They wanted to make sure the stent in his heart was in good shape and he was stable enough to be transferred. We still had some medical issues to contend with, but none of them seemed like a big deal after everything Grant had already overcome.

The biggest issue was that Grant's heel still wasn't healing. He had an open cast so doctors could treat the wound, and it required more acute care than Children's Hospital could provide. We would have to bring Grant back and forth to Harbor-UCLA for follow-up. Grant also had strange lumps all over his legs. In response to all his fractures, his body was overproducing calcium. This resulted in lumpy calcium deposits. Thankfully, they weren't dangerous. If they didn't go away on their own, they could be treated later.

After the CAT scan, Grant and I went back up to his room to wait for the results. He wasn't allowed to eat anything that morning before the test, and he was hungry and irritable. I finally gave in and gave him half a muffin, which he quickly ate before falling asleep. The doctor came in moments later. "There's a problem," he told me, holding out the scans.

"What is it?" For some reason, my mind immediately jumped to an administrative issue. Maybe the hospital had lost Grant's discharge papers or there had been a mix-up and Children's Hospital didn't have room for him after all.

"A pseudoaneurysm."

"What?" I covered my mouth with my hand, knowing that waking Grant was a surefire way to summon the Hulk.

"He formed calcium deposits around one of his groin arteries," the doctor explained, and my heart sunk. I knew this meant we weren't moving forward after all. At least not yet.

Luckily, Dr. Donayre was available to do the surgery to repair the artery, but since Grant had eaten that measly half of a muffin, we had to wait eight hours before he could operate. I went down to my car and brought up all of Grant's things, and then I called and canceled the ambulance.

Dr. Donayre came in at ten o'clock that night to perform the surgery. "Okay, Mom, you know the drill," he told me with a smile. "You take a break while I'm taking good care of your son."

I was grateful that Grant's life was once again in such capable hands, but my focus was elsewhere. "How long until we can transfer him?" I asked.

Dr. Donayre smiled again. "Let's see how the surgery goes first," he told me. "It shouldn't be more than a couple of weeks."

At this stage, a couple of weeks felt like a lifetime. It had been two months since the accident. Two months of living in horrible limbo without being able to plan a week or a day or even a moment into the future. Now that we were finally making progress, it felt like we were taking two steps back.

It didn't even occur to me until Grant was already in surgery that his life was in danger. This was major surgery. It involved almost all the same risks as the first time Dr. Donayre had placed the stent. But this time I felt completely confident. I knew we hadn't come this far to lose Grant on the operating table. Not when we still had so much further to go.

Grant got through the surgery fine, which was a huge relief, but the next two weeks were as difficult as I'd feared. Grant had to go back to a tiny, crowded corner of the ICU. As soon as he was stable and no longer sedated, Grant grew increasingly impatient and irritable. He thrashed around in his bed, trying to pull out his IV.

If John or one of the nurses got in his way, it didn't stop Grant, but he was completely different around Mackenzie and me. When Mackenzie came to visit, Grant's entire personality changed. A huge, goofy smile took over his face, and he repeated, "I love you, I love you," as she sat there holding his hand. This affectionate doting was a new side to Grant's personality, and a wonderful sign that maybe he really would come out of this better than ever.

When we finally got to Children's Hospital Los Angeles, we settled Grant into his room and met his main doctor, Kevan Craig, the director of rehabilitative medicine. I told Dr. Craig about everything we'd done to supplement Grant's care in the hospital. "That's wonderful," he said when I told him about the smoothies and essential oils. I was happy to see how open and responsive he was to these alternative treatments. "Your involvement going forward will be crucial to Grant's recovery."

I eyed Grant's file, which Dr. Craig was holding under his arm. It was at least three inches thick, and I wondered how long it would take Dr. Craig to read through all of it. "Oh, one other thing," I said. "Grant is on twenty grams of fish oil. I'd like him to continue at that dose."

Dr. Craig didn't bat an eye. "No problem. I'll make a note of it," he said, leaving us at the door to Grant's room.

Besides his temper, Grant's short-term memory was one of my greatest concerns. He clearly remembered John, Bryce, Mackenzie, and me, but he didn't recall what we told him from one moment to the next. I could tell that he was frustrated by his inability to remember the simplest things, like where he was or why we couldn't go home yet.

I was hopeful that the increased dose of fish oil would speed his brain's healing process and improve his memory, and I racked my brain for anything else I could do to help. During his first day at Children's Hospital, I gave Grant his phone back, hoping that scrolling through pictures and even social media accounts would help trigger his memory.

I was in a deep sleep in my bed at the condo the next night when my cell phone rang. I answered it without checking first to see who it was. "Hello?" My voice was husky with sleep.

"Mom," a halting voice said, "it's me."

I paused for a moment. "Grant?" I pulled the phone away from my ear to look at the screen. Sure enough, it read his name.

"Mom," he said again, his tone more urgent this time. "Do you know my name means warrior?" I nodded my head silently, fighting back tears. He really had heard me talking to him the whole time he was in the coma. He'd always been there. "I am Grant, I am a warrior," he said with a small laugh.

"Yes, you are, baby," I told him, wiping away the tears. "Yes, you are."

When I got to the hospital in the morning, a nurse was checking Grant's vitals as he stared off into space. "I had the strangest dream last night," I told the nurse, bending down to brush Grant's hair, which was finally growing back, away from his face. "I dreamed that Grant called me and we had a whole conversation about his name. He was talking in full sentences," I said in wonder.

The nurse laughed. "That wasn't a dream," she told me. "He really did call you. I helped him find the right button to push."

I looked at Grant lying peacefully in his Posey Bed. One of the reasons we'd chosen Children's Hospital was this bed, which was designed for patients who are at risk of extreme injury from a fall or unassisted bed exit. In other words, patients like Grant who couldn't be trusted to get into and out of bed without hurting themselves. Grant still couldn't walk, but the Posey Bed was there to keep everyone, including Grant, safe whenever the Hulk made an appearance. The bed zipped shut around him like a tent or, more aptly, a cage.

As I looked at Grant now, it was hard to imagine that we would ever need to protect ourselves from him. He stared up at me with an innocent expression and his new, slightly goofy grin. But there was barely any warning before the Hulk came out. Grant went from docile to violent in an instant. The doctors had a cocktail on hand at all times if they needed to sedate him. It was a potent mixture of Haldol, Ativan, and Benadryl that would calm Grant down with one shot, but keeping him tranquilized too much of the time didn't allow his brain to heal. It was another dance that we improvised as time went on.

Despite Grant's temper, the physical therapists, speech therapists, and occupational therapists got to work with him right away. The cast on his left leg and the screw sticking out of his heel prevented Grant from bearing any weight on his lower body, but the therapists did what they could. Grant was stable enough to get around in a regular wheelchair, so John and I helped Grant stand, supporting him with all of our strength before lowering him back down into the wheelchair. Then we were free to wheel him around the hospital for his various therapy sessions and frequent trips outside.

It didn't take long to see that the Hulk came out whenever Grant was tired or overstimulated. In so many ways, he was like an infant again, easily growing overstimulated by everything he was doing and learning. At first Grant could do his therapy for only five minutes at a time before he had to lie down for twenty. When he got overstimulated we zipped him into his bed, lowered the lights, and kept the room as quiet as possible to try to calm him down.

It seemed like everything overwhelmed and frustrated Grant, especially when he tried to remember things or perform tasks even slightly beyond his abilities. He was fine lifting hand weights in physical therapy to increase his upper-body strength, but when he moved on to throwing beanbags at a tick-tack-toe board, he quickly grew frustrated by his inability to hit the target. In occupational therapy, he spent days drawing a flower that looked like a three-year-old had drawn it.

Speech therapy, though, was by far the most daunting. Grant had a difficult time recalling words and couldn't remember the most basic facts, even ones about him. On his first day, the therapist asked him, "What's your name?"

He had to think for a minute. "Grant," he finally said, sounding very unsure.

The therapist wrote it down in big block letters—GRANT. "What does this say?" she asked him, but Grant just stared blankly at the page.

It was often in the midst of a benign moment such as this one when I would notice a line appearing on Grant's forehead, and I knew we were about to get a visit from the Hulk. We had to act fast and give him the cocktail before rushing him back to zip him up in his bed.

At first we didn't always notice the signs quickly enough, and

John almost always bore the brunt of Grant's temper. During a fit one day, Grant ripped John's shirt off. After another week John had scratches and bruises on his upper arm and a scab on his elbow from his run-ins with the Hulk.

We tried to keep Grant's nails trimmed as short as possible, but he fought us off whenever we approached him with the nail scissors. John finally managed to wrap his entire body around Grant to hold him down while I quickly cut his nails. I hated the fact that I was a little bit scared of him.

Eventually the hospital decided to station a security guard outside Grant's room and posted a sign on the door that read, "Please check with nurse before entering the room." Soon afterward, the security guard held a training session to teach the rest of the staff how to handle Grant. They were used to treating children with brain injuries, but most of the children weren't as big or as combative as Grant. During the lesson, Grant got frustrated at being manhandled and lunged at the security guard, ripping his pants.

After that, several of the nurses began to remove themselves from Grant's care. We were desperate to find a way to keep Grant at Children's Hospital, but of course we didn't want to put the nurses or other staff members in danger. In addition to the twenty-four-hour security guard, either John or I had to be present at Grant's bedside every moment that Grant was awake.

Meanwhile, Grant's speech was coming back slowly. He'd progressed from "Let's go" to "I want to go home." He repeated that sentence over and over again. "I want to go home. When can we go home?"

John and I had agreed on an explanation, which we recited to Grant many times a day. "There are some medical things we have to take care of here that we can't manage at home," we told him. "As soon as those things are under control, we can go home."

Grant always seemed to accept this in the moment. Then a minute later he would ask, "When can we go home?" John or I would explain the situation again, and then a minute or two later Grant would say, "I want to go home." This went on all day long.

Despite Grant's desire to go home, it seemed at times that he was actively working against his own recovery. His heel was still a major issue. Despite the doctors' best efforts, it wasn't healing well. The open cast allowed the doctors access to the wound, which still held pieces of bone and debris, but unfortunately this also gave access to Grant. Sometimes when he was lying in bed, he opened the bandages and messed around with the wound. No matter how many times we told him to stop, he refused.

When Bryce was visiting, he calmly told Grant, "Dude, that's gross. Leave it alone so it can get better." I thought this might finally do the trick—Grant had been responding so well to Bryce so far. But as he looked at Bryce, I saw the line developing on Grant's forehead.

"Don't tell me what to do!" Grant hollered. I took a deep breath and immediately zipped the bed shut around him.

"What an idiot," Bryce said, shaking his head. "Doesn't he know that we're trying to help him?"

I looked at Grant, thrashing around in his Posey Bed. "No, honey," I told Bryce. "I don't think he does."

The next morning Grant was doing physical therapy when I got to Children's Hospital. "Hi, honey," I said as I walked into the room. He was sitting in his wheelchair holding on to two huge ropes that were attached to the wall. Swinging the ropes up and down as if they were jump ropes helped build his upper body strength.

Grant stopped what he was doing and looked at me. "I want my mom," he said slowly.

I took a step closer to him. "I'm right here, honey," I said calmly. Despite his memory issues, Grant had always recognized me.

"No!" Grant screamed with a ferocious look on his face. "I want my real mom!"

By then, I had been holding it together for over three months. Since the first twenty-four hours after the accident, I hadn't really lost it. Sure, I'd choked up at his bedside plenty of times, and on a few occasions I'd cried myself to sleep at the Residence Inn, but I hadn't publicly let go. This, however, was just too much for me to take.

I turned around so that Grant wouldn't see me cry and almost walked right into a nurse who had just entered the room. She had heard everything. As she silently stepped toward me I let myself fall into her arms, and she held on to me tightly as I sobbed.

As the days passed, I felt myself growing as frustrated as Grant. In therapy, I could tell that we could push him harder, but the therapists warned me to back off in case my encouragement sent Grant over the edge. I often got calls from the hospital late at night when Grant had an outburst. One night I was trying to sleep when my phone rang. I answered it and heard people screaming and things crashing to the ground. It sounded like the end of the world. But when I arrived at the hospital, Grant was sedated and everything was back to normal.

The doctors kept assuring John and me that Grant's temper was typical of someone coming out of a coma, but that did little to allay my fears. *What if this is the end of the road? What if we've awakened a monster?*

It was impossible to tell how much of Grant's aggression stemmed from his brain injury and how much of it was his bipolar disorder rearing its head. Grant had never been this violent, but his bipolar disorder had made him aggressive and angry at times before the accident. As Grant's brain healed, it gradually returned to its old self. We had to constantly adjust his meds in our efforts to control for the bipolar disorder while treating the brain injury.

There were plenty of good things happening too, and when Thanksgiving came just a couple of weeks after Grant arrived at Children's Hospital, I made sure to give thanks for all of them. I was grateful that Grant never got angry with Mackenzie. She visited often and sat in the Posey Bed with Grant for hours, holding his hand and talking to him softly. If Mackenzie was there, Grant had a huge grin on his face. During these times, I was so grateful for Mackenzie. She was only sixteen, and her loyalty to Grant was a gift to all of us.

Now when I played blackjack with Grant, he knew when to hold and when to double down. I was grateful for this sign that his recall was improving. Meanwhile, everything seemed to be planned perfectly for the book launch, and I was thankful for everyone on my team who had worked so hard to make that launch happen successfully despite the circumstances.

On Thanksgiving Day, John picked up Bryce and drove him to the hospital to be with us while I went out to Whole Foods to buy a turkey breast and some roasted veggies. The four of us sat in the hospital room eating our prepared turkey off paper plates. Grant was in his bed, and the rest of us were sitting on uncomfortable hospital chairs.

It was not the way Norman Rockwell would have portrayed the holiday, but Grant was calm, and Bryce was happy. We were together, and we had so much to be thankful for. It was one of the best holidays I could remember sharing with them in a long time.

TAKING CARE OF YOUR FAMILY MEANS TAKING CARE OF YOURSELF!
Get quick tips to make it easier at www.WarriorMomBook.com/tips.

7

He's Not Ready

I was in a small hotel gym in Maryland when I got a call from my agent and publisher. "Congratulations!" They cheered into the phone. "*The Virgin Diet* is officially a *New York Times* bestseller."

The book had been released just a few days after Thanksgiving, and I left for a two-week public television tour. John stepped in and stayed at Grant's bedside while I was gone. It was difficult and disorienting to go from the intensity of the hospital to the completely different type of intensity of the tour.

I traveled from city to city for pledge drives, feeling lonely and disconnected from what was going on with both of my sons. Bryce was at home, Grant was in the hospital, and I was alone on the road trying to focus on my job but constantly wondering what was going on with each of them. When the cameras started rolling, I had to compartmentalize and turn it on, and I often heard myself speaking passionately about *The Virgin Diet* while picturing Bryce alone at home or Grant in his bed playing with the wound on his heel.

Here it was, the moment I'd been working and hoping for all this time, and I was numb. "What number?" I asked, and they told me that the book would debut at number six on the bestseller list. "Okay, thanks," I said in a voice that sounded flat even to me. I didn't believe in the Virgin Diet any less, but everything felt so mundane after months of dealing with life-and-death stakes.

"JJ, this is amazing," my agent reminded me. "You did it! Do you know how many books make it onto the bestseller list?"

I took a deep breath and wiped the sweat off my forehead with a small hotel towel. "You're right," I told her. "Thank you." I stepped back onto the StairMaster, grateful for this wake-up call. *I did it.* I paused for a moment of gratitude before launching back into action. To me, this was a good start. I was glad that the book was succeeding, and especially that it was helping so many people, but my next thought was *What can I do to reach more people and get it to number one?* I knew the book could have an even bigger impact. Instead of taking a moment to celebrate my win, I was determined to better my best.

When I got back to the hospital a few days later, it was as if I had never left. Day after day, the rehab team at Children's Hospital worked with Grant, trying to help him regain his memory, his cognition, and his ability to do countless essential tasks, from talking to tying his shoes to brushing his teeth. Grant was supposed to be in therapy for three hours a day, but all of his therapists knew that when the Hulk showed up, therapy was over.

Despite this, Grant was progressing quickly. After getting back from the public television tour, I joined Grant in speech therapy. "Do you know your name?" the young speech therapist asked him.

"Grant Virgin," he said automatically.

"Very good," she praised him as she pulled out a small whiteboard and a black marker. "Can you spell it?"

I looked at Grant, nervously anticipating an appearance from the Hulk. I didn't think he was anywhere close to being able to spell yet. "G-R-A-N-T V-I-R-G-I-N," he responded quickly.

"Very good," the therapist repeated as she wrote something down on her board. "How old are you?" she asked, pointing to the numbers she had written: 16.

Grant paused, staring at the board. "Grant Virgin," he repeated stiffly. He didn't know the answer. I could feel his disappointment in every part of my body.

Besides his violent temper and cognitive issues, the other main symptom of Grant's brain injury fell on the opposite end of the spectrum—hysterical, uncontrollable laughter. This laughter often came at inappropriate times, such as in the middle of a therapy session or when one of us reprimanded him for acting out. It was all part of his regaining his reflexes, but it was still contagious and boosted our spirits, often when we really needed it.

Children's Hospital had a bathing room, where a patient in a wheelchair could take a bubble bath. After carefully wrapping Grant's heel so it wouldn't get wet, I brought him in there. As soon as he saw the bubbles, Grant erupted into laughter, which continued to grow louder and louder as he tried to pop the bubbles and throw them in my direction.

My mind flashed to an image of Grant and Bryce as toddlers in the bathtub together. One of the best things about their being so close in age was putting them in the tub together each night. No matter how much they'd fought or whined throughout the day, bath time was always fun. The two made Santa Claus beards on each other with the bubbles and pretended the white foam was snow. Looking at Grant now, I felt as if no time had passed. He was the same little boy in the damaged body of a grown man.

Bryce visited again that weekend, and he and Grant watched the movie *Beavis and Butt-Head Do America*. Grant was in his bed, but he wasn't touching his heel and seemed more focused than usual on what was happening on the screen. I was working on my laptop and not really paying attention to the movie until something happened that made Bryce and Grant laugh at the exact same time. Grant's laugh was louder and less controlled than Bryce's, but when I looked up at them laughing together, they looked like any two brothers just hanging out and watching a movie.

This laughter at an appropriate time, for once, was one of the first signs that Grant was starting to get his social cues back. From then on, the Hulk came out less and less, and when he did, Grant always apologized. "I'm so sorry, I'm so sorry," he repeated after snapping out of it.

The best thing to happen that month was that Grant's heel finally started to get better. When the cast came off, it was a monumental event. We hadn't seen Grant's left foot since the night of the accident. The orthopedist brought a small handheld saw into Grant's zippered bed and carefully sliced the cast away. He then used a pair of scissors to cut through the bandages around Grant's lower leg and foot.

The muscles in Grant's leg had atrophied and his calf was far skinnier than mine, but the skin looked intact and beautiful. The orthopedist handed me the cast, which was caked with dried blood, small pieces of scab, and debris. "Good riddance," I said as I held it up for one last look before tossing it right into the garbage.

With the cast off, Grant could finally try to walk. At this point, he'd been bedridden for well over three months. It took several nurses to help Grant stand for the first time, and he wobbled back and forth precariously before having to sit back down. For a while, standing up for just a moment required all of Grant's strength and concentration, but it got easier and easier.

He progressed like a baby, starting by pulling himself up to stand before cruising while holding on to furniture and then finally trying to walk. After only a few days without the cast, Grant was able to walk about ten feet while leaning on a walker with two therapists holding on to him.

Grant still didn't remember the therapists from one day to the next, but as his aggression lessened, Grant grew more polite and pleasant to be around. "Thank you," he said to each therapist when his or her shift was over. He smiled at the other patients and even waved when he passed one of them in the brightly colored hallway.

We still didn't know if Grant would ever be able to walk on his own, but now that the cast was off, it seemed like a good time to start him on aquatic therapy. I'd used water exercise for my own rehab from surgeries and sports injuries and was sure that Grant would benefit from being in the water. Children's Hospital didn't have a pool, but they did have a large hydrotherapy tank. When I brought it up with Dr. Craig, he told me, "He's not ready." He was concerned that Grant might have an outburst in the water and put himself in danger.

John and I weren't going to accept this. The condo where I was staying had a full-sized pool, and in mid-December we decided to bring Grant there. It was his first time on furlough since the accident. Getting Grant out of the wheelchair and into the car and then out of the car and back into the wheelchair was difficult even with Bryce, John, and me all working together, but as soon as we got Grant into the pool, he took off like a fish, swimming full, perfectly executed strokes under the water. In awe, I pulled out my camera and took a video of Grant walking effortlessly across the pool in the water while laughing hysterically and wearing an enormous smile.

It did Grant good to feel, just for a moment, as if he could do anything that a normal person could. From that point on, I could sense that his attitude had shifted. He finally believed in himself, and this sped up his progress more than anything else. Soon he was walking farther, tying his shoes, and even feeding himself.

Now that those skills were taken care of, Grant's therapists used toys and games to keep him motivated. In occupational therapy, Grant played a game of Connect 4. The therapist held a red disk far above Grant's head, forcing him to stretch his arm up to grab it. He reached up as far as he could and had to wiggle his fingers to grasp the disk. On his next turn, the therapist held a red piece up for him again. Grant looked up at it and then darted his eyes to the table beside him where the game box was sitting. He reached into the box and snatched a different red disk.

"Did you just cheat?" the therapist asked good-naturedly. With a grin, Grant leaned back in his chair, nodded proudly, and sputtered into laughter. Everyone in the room joined in. It felt so good to see my Grant outsmarting people once again.

As Grant's awareness grew, he was able to remember where he was, but he'd never forgotten where he wanted to be. "I want to go home" were still the words Grant spoke the most frequently. Now that he was having fewer outbursts, we tried to use this desire to motivate him in therapy.

"The better we do with the therapists, the sooner we can go home," John and I repeated to Grant over and over.

Grant nodded, continued on with his therapy, and then asked again a moment later, "When can I go home?" I got calls from Grant late at night. "Mom, when can I go home?" he demanded. Finally we made a chart that listed everything that needed to happen before we could go home.

"Fewer outbursts" was written at the top of the chart. The Hulk had already gone from appearing two or three times a day to only once every few days. One thing that seemed to help whenever Grant got frustrated or overwhelmed was drawing. In occupational therapy, his drawings had gone from toddler-style scribbles to complex works of art. Drawing helped Grant focus and gave him an outlet to express himself when he so often couldn't find the right words. I was pleasantly shocked to see this evidence of Grant's artistic side. He had never shown any interest in art before.

Grant's therapists also noted his desire to work on his art and used it to motivate him to reach his other goals. The physical therapists took him the long way around the hospital, making him walk farther than necessary to the art room. The occupational therapists asked Grant to draw more complex images, forcing him to stretch his cognitive abilities and fine motor skills.

All of these techniques helped Grant continue to make great strides. By Christmas he could dress himself, walk with only a little bit of support from his walker, and throw and catch a ball. My emotional state fluctuated between hugely grateful and positive, thinking of every step forward as a win, and terrified about where Grant would end up. What would the rest of his life look like?

On Christmas Day when Bryce got to the hospital for a visit, Grant was able to walk down the hallway with his walker to greet him. "Whoa, dude. Look at you," Bryce said from several feet away. It was the first time he'd seen Grant walk since the accident. "Let's go outside," Bryce said. Being in the hospital on Christmas Day was depressing. We decided to go for a walk at the Grove, an outdoor mall near the condo I'd rented.

As we slowly walked around outside admiring the Christmas decorations, I held back for a minute and watched Grant and Bryce walking ahead of me. Grant leaned on his walker and still had a limp, but they were walking in sync, with their heads bent toward each other.

"How was that?" I asked Bryce when I finally caught up with them.

"It was weird," Bryce said with a smile that told me how relieved he was to be getting his brother back.

Later that day, I took the boys back to the condo for dinner. I had a surprise waiting there for Grant—our dog, Daisy. Grant had always adored Daisy, and I wondered why he hadn't asked for her yet. He hadn't seen her since the night of the accident. I held my breath as we walked into the room, worried that Grant wouldn't remember her. Daisy immediately came bounding toward us, barking happily, her tail wagging at a feverish pace.

"Daisy!" Grant dropped to his knees as Daisy jumped up to lick him all over his face.

After dinner we took Grant outside to swim in the pool. For the second time I saw the way he came fully alive in the water— not only physically, but also emotionally, even spiritually. The self-assuredness and poise that came over him was something I hadn't seen in a long time, if ever before.

Watching Grant in the pool, I realized that we had it backward. Instead of waiting to bring Grant home until his outbursts completely ended, maybe his outbursts would end when we finally brought him home. Even with his limited language, he'd been telling us for quite some time what he really wanted. What if his violent episodes were in part a reaction to being kept in the hospital against his will?

After the holiday, John and I met with the doctors to discuss the possibility of bringing Grant home. They were unanimously against it, arguing that this was a crucial time in Grant's recovery, and removing him from the hospital now would interrupt his progress.

"He's not ready," they argued yet again. But John and I wondered if it would be better to find a team of therapists who could treat Grant at home, in the comfort of familiar surroundings. It was also clear that aquatic therapy, which we could also arrange at home, would be enormously helpful, but the hospital wasn't willing to start Grant on aquatic therapy until the outbursts ended completely.

At this point, Grant was medically stable and functioning pretty well. He could dress himself, brush his teeth, and go to the bathroom by himself. That was more than he was able to do independently back when he'd started preschool! His speech and cognitive function still had a ways to go, but I was confident that we could work on those things at home.

Once again we found ourselves going against what the doctors thought was best for Grant, but I was confident that no one knew my son or what was right for him better than I did. It was time to throw out the chart and start on a whole new course.

ARE YOU A WARRIOR MOM?

Find out at www.WarriorMomBook.com/quiz.

8

Don't Wish It Were Easier,
Make Yourself Stronger

In early January, John and Bryce brought Grant home from Children's Hospital. They arrived at our house in Palm Desert to find balloons lining the driveway and a banner across our front door reading, "Welcome Home, Grant!" Our whole neighborhood was lined up along the sidewalk to celebrate Grant's return.

I wasn't there. Grant's initial homecoming coincided with an appearance on the *Today* show and some other media to promote *The Virgin Diet*, which had surprised everyone by staying on the *New York Times* bestseller list for all but one week in December. A part of me felt incredibly guilty. How could I miss my son's homecoming after being in the hospital for months? But my publisher and I were counting on the *Today* show appearance to drive sales. If I missed it and the book didn't continue to succeed, we'd have even bigger problems.

The shift from spending my days in the hospital to being in Manhattan to promote *The Virgin Diet* felt lonely and surreal. It was so quiet in my hotel room, and a part of me missed the buzz and constant hum of activity in the hospital. Most of all, I missed Grant. Besides the public television tour, I had been by his side day in and day out for over four months. Being separated from him now, just as he arrived back at home, felt like being torn in two. John texted me dozens of videos and pictures of Grant at home sitting on the couch with Mackenzie and cuddling with Daisy. Each text cheered me up and made me homesick at the same time.

I still had no idea exactly how much all of Grant's medical care would ultimately cost, but the bills were beginning to pile up. I'd seen only a few tallies: $30,000 for the helicopter ride from Palm Desert to Palm Springs, and then an additional $82,000 to fly Grant to the hospital in Torrance. That didn't even begin to cover Grant's four months of inpatient care, most of which was spent in the ICU. I knew my insurance would pay for a lot of these costs, but I would still owe tens of thousands of dollars.

I tried not to think about these numbers. I certainly didn't have the money to pay these bills, but Grant couldn't have afforded not to receive all that care. I would happily have gone broke if that had been the only way to get him the services that he needed to save his life. Now I was more motivated than ever to be successful so Grant could continue to receive whatever therapy and treatments he needed at home.

I soon found that in every interview about the book, people wanted to talk about Grant. But I wasn't ready to talk about Grant yet. "Your agent told me that you launched this book while your son was in a coma," one of the *Today* show producers told me while I was getting ready in the greenroom for my appearance. I nodded slightly as the makeup artist brushed blush onto my cheeks.

"That's amazing," she told me. "You know, the day after I heard that, I found out that my landlord is selling the building I live in. I'm in the middle of planning a wedding, and now I have to find a new place to live and move out within a month." I didn't say anything. I wasn't sure what this had to do with Grant or me. "I started freaking out," she continued, "but then I told myself, 'That woman JJ Virgin launched a bestseller while her son was in a coma! She went through ten times this amount of stress. If she could pull that off, then I can handle this.'"

I just stared at this woman, who stood there looking so beautiful and poised. Was it possible that she had really gained strength from me? As I went from one appearance to the next, producers, hosts, and even readers echoed her sentiments. "Your story inspired me," they told me. "It gave me strength. How did you do it?"

I wasn't ready to answer these questions yet, so I always steered the conversation back to *The Virgin Diet* and then rushed back to my hotel room to be alone and think. I didn't want to say it, but the truth was, I didn't know how I had done it. I had just done it. Every morning that Grant was in the hospital, I'd woken up terrified of what the day in front of me would hold. A huge part of me wanted to pull the covers over my eyes and hide from the whole situation.

But of course I couldn't. Grant needed me. So I got up and put one foot in front of the other and did whatever I had to do until the day was done. Then I did it all over again. I had no grand plan, no secret angel whispering directions into my ear—at least, none that I was aware of. But now that so many people were asking me how I'd done it, I felt a need to put the pieces of the puzzle together so the process could be replicated.

There was no time to put it all together yet. I was still in the thick of it. When I got home from New York, it felt like returning to a battle scene. The first time I drove around our neighborhood, I saw signs on nearly every lawn reading, "Slow down. We love our children." I had to pull over to the side of the road to catch my breath. A wound that had just barely started to heal had ripped open.

Grant was home, but not full-time. In early January, we had reached a compromise with Children's Hospital—until the end of the month, Grant would go to a rehabilitation center in Los Angeles during the week for therapy and go home on the weekends. After I got home from New York, John and I took turns bringing Grant back and forth between the rehab center and home while working to set up a team to take over Grant's care when he was able to move back home full-time.

We had seen how beneficial it was for the team at Children's Hospital to work collaboratively. Throughout Grant's stay there, John and I attended regular meetings with his nurses, occupational therapists, physical therapists, psychiatrist, social worker, neurologist, and orthopedist. Together they created the best program for Grant and tweaked that program frequently based on one another's feedback. What was happening with Grant neurologically affected his progress in physical therapy and vice versa.

His treatment could not be compartmentalized, and in those meetings I was impressed by the way everyone's opinions held equal weight. It didn't matter if an idea came from a physical therapist or the director of rehabilitation. Everyone in the room was able to set ego aside and put their ideas together to create the best plan for Grant.

John and I were determined to re-create this dynamic at home, and by the end of January, we had everything in place—an outpatient medical team as well as a psychiatrist, speech therapist, and physical therapist. John went to the rehabilitation center and gathered Grant's things. On the way home, they stopped at the Harbor-UCLA Medical Center, where Grant had stayed for the first two months after his accident. We wanted the nurses and doctors to see how far Grant had come since he'd left.

It had been just over two months since Grant had left there in a wheelchair, combative and barely conscious. Now he walked into the hospital with only a slight limp and hugged each staff member with a proud smile on his face.

"You are a miracle," one of the nurses said, reaching up to pat Grant gently on the cheek. At this point, you could hardly tell that anything was wrong. He was strong and tall, and his hair had grown so much that he looked like a typical teenage boy in need of a haircut. But there were issues lurking beneath the surface. Grant still needed to undergo a follow-up knee surgery. He struggled to find the right words, his sentences running in circles as he relied on simple words like "thing" and "place" over and over. Most troubling, though, was the way Grant so easily grew angry and frustrated by his own limitations. I hoped that being surrounded by friends and family would help him progress faster at home.

Unfortunately, that's not what happened. Coming home wasn't the end of the journey; it was just the beginning. Grant walked into the house, put his walker away, and went straight to his room to play video games. At Children's Hospital he'd been motivated to do well in therapy by the promise of coming home, and we could no longer use that desire to get him up and moving. He spent all of his time drawing or playing video games. We attempted to use the same techniques they had in the hospital—hiding the remote so he had to get up every time he wanted to change the channel or start a new game and moving his art supplies across the house so he had to walk farther to get them—but it didn't have the same effect.

Grant was also struggling socially. While Mackenzie and his other friends had been great about sending cards and visiting when he was in the hospital, they didn't know how to relate to Grant once he was home. He was socially awkward and unable to think of the right words to keep up with the flow of conversation. Like a toddler, he felt it was all about him. He wanted to do what he wanted to do and talk about whatever interested him, which changed from one moment to the next. He just didn't fit in with his old friends anymore.

I didn't blame Mackenzie or his other friends when they stopped calling and visiting the house, but it pained me to see Grant so isolated. Bryce had tons of friends who often came by the house to hang out. It struck me how independent Bryce had grown over the past few months. He'd been basically fending for himself since the accident. Grant often tried to hang out with Bryce and his friends, but he still easily grew overstimulated. When he couldn't keep pace with them he retreated to his room, slamming the door behind him.

The doctors had warned us that because of physical changes in the brain and the patient's struggle to adjust to a new life with limited abilities, depression is one of the most common long-lasting symptoms of a brain injury. Grant's bipolar disorder made this even more complex and difficult. He had no patience and no filter. The sounds of his screaming at us to leave him alone and the slamming of doors became our home's background noise. When Bryce wasn't with his friends, he was holed up in his room, hiding from Grant just as he had when they were younger.

Though he'd fought so hard to get out of the hospital, now that he was home it seemed like all Grant wanted was to go back there. After his knee surgery, Grant wasn't supposed to walk on that leg at all, but he did anyway. Of course, this left him in a lot of pain, and he demanded to go to the hospital. When I told him to wait, he decided to walk there himself in his bare feet, just like on the night of the accident. I couldn't physically hold him back, but it was too dangerous to let him wander around alone, so I called the paramedics and they brought him home. Grant responded by swallowing a handful of pills, so we ended up back in the hospital after all.

Just a few nights later, Grant had another outburst over seemingly nothing and threatened to take more pills. I chased after him into the bathroom and stopped him just in time—he had two prescription bottles in his hands. "Grant, no," I shouted, struggling to wrestle the bottles out of his hands. He was stronger and faster than me. He pushed me off and darted around me, running through the house and out the front door. John was just pulling up the driveway in his car, and as Grant slowed down to avoid the car, I managed to pin him against its side. John realized what was going on and jumped out of the car, and the two of us held him there as John finally managed to get the pills away from Grant.

"Bryce!" I screamed at the top of my lungs. He was hiding in his room, as usual. He came outside, looking worried. "Call 911," I told him as I held Grant firmly against the car, both of us panting for air.

The thought that ran through my mind day in and day out was *When will this end?* Just like Grant, I felt isolated and alone. Whether we agreed with them or not, at least in the hospital we were surrounded by people we could turn to with questions. At home we had no support. Worst of all, Grant's progress was beginning to plateau, and I was once more filled with doubt about whether we'd made the right decision. Maybe he would have been better off staying in the hospital longer after all. He wasn't happy there, but at least he was progressing and he was safe.

The only way I got through this was by telling myself that I hadn't exhausted all of my resources. There was still more that could be done, so I kept searching for new solutions. When I told Grant's psychiatrist about the pills, the outbursts, and the isolation, she referred us to a speech-language pathologist named Marcey Utter.

Marcey has a kind face and a big smile, and always seems to be in a good mood. In truth, she is much more than a speech therapist. Equal parts enthusiastic and patient, she knew just how to navigate Grant's moods and keep him motivated. She specializes in working with kids on the autism spectrum, so she focused a lot of her work on developing social skills. This was just what Grant needed, and I was relieved to see how comfortable Grant seemed with Marcey from the very beginning. They just clicked, and Marcey quickly became Grant's one and only friend and confidante.

Marcey started her work with Grant by going over categories of things to try to get his memory back and create new files in his head to replace the ones wiped out or buried after the accident. She held up a picture of a red apple with the word "apple" written under it. "Is this something you eat or something you drink?"

Grant stared at the image. "Thing you eat," he said after a moment. Marcey smiled.

"Very good," she told him. "What is it called?" She pointed again to the word.

Grant stared at the image of the apple again. I could see how hard he was trying to remember. "Thing you eat," he said again, looking down at his shoes.

I struggled to know what to say to Grant in these moments. I had been his cheerleader for so long—and would of course continue to play that role—but his disappointment filled me with despair. No matter how many times I told him that he was going to come out of this better than ever, I could tell that he didn't really believe me. I'll admit that when I had to wrestle pills out of his hands and call the paramedics for help, it was hard for me to keep believing it too.

• • •

Around this time, I hosted my first official Mindshare Summit. I was really excited about this summit, which was an opportunity for some of the top wellness experts from around the country to gather together to support one another and share ideas about how to grow our businesses. We had some great people lined up to speak and attend, and I was eager to find ways to help them get their messages out in a bigger way.

I was keenly aware that Grant's survival was thanks in part to my connections within the wellness community. Without them, I wouldn't have known about essential oils, progesterone, or fish oil, which had all played a role in his recovery. I wanted every family that went through something like this to have access to this information, and helping these health leaders expand their brands was my way of making this happen.

On the day of the event I was a bundle of nerves. Just the day before, Grant had had an outburst because he wanted to stay home alone while I was at the summit. I knew how frustrating it must have been for a teenager previously used to having plenty of independence to be treated like a child, but the fact was, at that point he wasn't safe in the house alone. When I told him as much, he stormed out of the house in his bare feet yet again.

I walked into the hotel where we were holding the event, took a breath, and tried to put all of that behind me. John was with Grant, and I could focus on where I was right now. In the conference room, I looked around at the sixty health professionals who were gathered. These were doctors doing groundbreaking work, bestselling authors, and various other health and wellness entrepreneurs. Our main speaker was Ali Brown, the business coach I'd hired years before to help me push forward in my career. The level of firepower in that room was amazing. Together we could really improve lives and change the world.

As everyone began introducing themselves and sharing a bit about their histories, I realized something. Nearly every person in that room had been through a major trauma or obstacle in their lives and had not only survived but bounced back stronger than ever. There was Cynthia Pasquella, who'd gone from suffering from severe illness and thoughts of suicide to become a transformative nutritionist and one of the most vibrant people I knew; Dr. Alan Christianson, who was born with cerebral palsy and defied the odds to become a successful doctor and a competitive athlete; and Leanne Ely, a single mom who'd gone from selling cookbooks out of the trunk of her car to launching an online business and becoming a hugely successful entrepreneur.

Even my event director Pattie Ptak, who had helped me put together this event, had been in three car accidents in three months that had left her in terrible pain before she began a healing journey that led her to run a successful wellness center for eighteen years. During that time, she'd helped tens of thousands of people get healthy.

Though I'd spent plenty of time with most of these people before, I had never realized that we shared a history of trauma and challenges. I quickly thought about some of the other amazing entrepreneurs I knew who weren't in that room, and sure enough, each of them had faced a major tragedy or challenge in their lives too, whether it was abuse, poverty, illness, addiction, bankruptcy, or depression. We were the walking wounded, and yet somehow we weren't wounded at all. We were strong, confident, and brave. Had the tragedies we'd faced in our lives made us this way?

During lunch, I had a chance to talk to Alan Christianson and learn more about his story. Dr. Christianson told me that he was born with cerebral palsy and suffered from seizures for most of his early life. This left him with limited mobility and poor coordination. As he grew up, Dr. Christianson became obese as a result of his lack of physical activity. He was a stereotypical nerd, and he threw himself into his studies, reading encyclopedias to fill his lonely free time.

Dr. Christianson was in seventh grade when he became the target of a bully who started picking on him for being fat and slow. "This was a crushing moment," he told me, but instead of allowing his spirit to be crushed, Alan was motivated to reset his health and finally get in better physical shape.

Most of the people in his life didn't think this was possible. They believed that a child with cerebral palsy was destined to live an unhealthy, sedentary life. Dr. Christianson set out to prove them wrong. He was determined to stop being limited by the condition he was born with, and he began reading every book on nutrition, fitness, and health that he could get his hands on. Eventually he created his own recovery plan. He gave up sugar and processed foods and created an exercise plan that was easy enough for him to start on.

"At first I was in such bad shape that I could run only one lap around the kitchen," he told me. "But I stuck with it and built on it. Soon I was running ten laps around the kitchen, and then twenty laps. I added agility drills to improve my balance and so that I could cover more distance on foot." Just two years later, Dr. Christianson had become a varsity football player and his class's best endurance runner. This led him to a career in health. By the time he arrived at the Mindshare Summit, he had a thriving private practice and had written multiple books that were helping thousands of people.

"My past circumstances help me connect with my patients and feel what they're feeling," Dr. Christianson told me. "I'm grateful for my illness. If I hadn't gone through that, I would never be where I am today."

As we filed back into the conference room, I thought about Dr. Christianson's last statement. It was inspiring to think that he had become so successful not in spite of his challenges but because of them.

Ever since Grant had returned home, the one thing I'd been asked over and over was "How did you do it?" It struck me that the answer was connected to the fact that all the successful, inspiring people in this room had faced such big obstacles in their lives. Maybe all of us were better equipped to launch a new business or face the near death of a child because of the challenges we'd already faced. Those difficulties had forced us to step up and gain new capabilities and had increased our tolerance for stress. They had made us stronger.

Intrigued, I took my seat and began listing the greatest challenges I'd faced before Grant's accident. "Divorce" was at the top of the list, followed by "Dad's death" and "Grant's bipolar disorder." It wasn't difficult to see how dealing with each of these things had in many ways prepared me to face Grant's accident.

The divorce from John was incredibly painful. The fighting, the animosity, and the tug-of-war over the kids took a major toll on me and caused me to doubt myself time and time again. But now I could see that it had also taught me to trust my instincts. Deep down, I knew that John and I were not a good match despite how much I cared for him. I also knew what to fight for, especially when it came to my kids. Tuning in to that inner voice during that time prepared me to hear it on the night of the accident. When I wondered if we should listen to the doctors' advice and let Grant go, I got a clear hit that told me to move my feet. If I hadn't recognized that voice and learned to trust it, I might not have listened.

We were still in the midst of the ugliest part of the divorce when I got a call from my mom with the news I'd been dreading for years. My dad had been diagnosed with late-stage lung cancer and was expected to die within a year. My mother was shocked by this news, but I had to admit that I wasn't. My father was a heavy drinker and smoker and had had a terrible hacking cough for years.

My dad ended up living for three more years, and I made an effort to spend as much time with him as possible before he died. Before Grant's accident, this had been the hardest period of my life—battling over the divorce while working long hours to make ends meet and traveling back and forth to visit my sick father—but I also learned so much from this time.

Clearly my dad had been sick for a long time before he was diagnosed. Maybe there was something that could have been done to save him. This confirmed the importance of listening to my instincts. I didn't want to ever look back at my life and wish I'd tuned in and realized what was going on sooner, so I began a habit of starting every day by asking myself, *What are you pretending not to know?* This habit of taking a moment to check in with my instincts served me well after Grant's accident.

Living through my dad's battle with cancer also prepared me for the emotional roller coaster of Grant's recovery. I knew that I had to advocate for Grant, so I insisted on knowing every detail of what was going on with him while searching out every alternative treatment that had even the slightest possibility of helping him. Because his life was on the line, there was no stone I was going to leave unturned.

Then there was Grant. Long before the accident, he had always been my greatest challenge. The outbursts. The expulsions. The constant stress and worry. When he was young, I became so overwhelmed that I confessed to one of our many therapists, "I don't think I'm strong enough to handle this child."

The therapist looked me right in the eye. "Well, you have to handle him," he told me. "So how are we going to get you strong enough to do it?"

I hadn't realized that facing every challenge in my life was one long journey toward becoming strong enough.

• • •

A few days later, I was working out at the gym with Grant. I had finally found something that motivated him—the idea of being "big and strong"—so I took him to the gym with me as often as possible to lift weights, in addition to his physical therapy sessions. Slowly he had started to progress again. At speech therapy he could say the days of the week and the months of the year, and his vocabulary was slowly expanding. But his outbursts had continued as he fought for more independence.

Just as when he was in the hospital messing with the wound on his heel, it seemed that he was often working against his own best interests. I wished he could see that we would grant him more independence when we could trust him not to hurt himself.

That morning he was upset because he couldn't cook breakfast for himself. "It's not fair," he grunted as he lifted a barbell above his head. It was amazing to see how strong and agile he'd gotten. If only he'd put the same energy into his work with Marcey that he put into working out at the gym.

"Grant," I said as he began his next set of reps, "think about the muscles in your body. When you lift those weights, you're stressing the muscle and breaking down the muscle fibers." Grant just continued with what he was doing, but I could tell he was listening. "Your body then repairs the muscle fibers, which causes the muscle to grow."

Grant dropped the barbell and let his head hang forward, exhausted. "You are the same as your muscles," I told him. "The accident broke you down, but you can get stronger than ever by patching yourself back up again."

"What's the point?" Grant said, wiping his forehead with a towel.

"The point is to get better," I told him, "to get stronger. Think about all the things the doctors said you would never do." I ticked them off on my hands. "They said you'd never wake up, you'd never walk, you'd never talk, and now you're doing all of those things. If there's still more you want to do, then you have to keep fighting until you can," I told him.

Grant was silent for a moment, and then he looked at me. "It's too hard," he said quietly.

I thought about the roomful of people at the Mindshare Summit, all of whom had gone through such hardships to become the people they were today—successful, content professionals who were inspiring others and changing lives. They had been flexing the muscles they needed to strengthen in order to face obstacles since their childhoods, and this had prepared them for anything. Their challenges weren't burdens; they were opportunities.

I knew without a doubt that the same was true for Grant. I would have given anything to spare him from going through the pain of the accident, but I saw now that it was a gift. It was a chance for him to get stronger. Because he had survived this, there was nothing he wouldn't be able to do, no challenge too big for him to face. There were sure to be many more obstacles ahead of him, but each one would prepare him for the next, making him stronger, fiercer, and more powerful than ever.

Grant could choose to view each challenge he faced in the future as an opportunity or as a crisis. The work involved would be the same either way, but the outcome would be vastly different. I hoped more than anything that Grant would see every one of his challenges as a gift of opportunity.

I looked at Grant. His very presence was a miracle. That was the word—"miracle"—that people most often used to describe Grant's survival. And I certainly didn't disagree with this. But I now saw clearly that I had used all the lessons I'd learned throughout my life to help make this miracle happen.

The ups and downs of my life had taught me that there is always light at the end of even the darkest tunnels. I knew how to hold on to hope even when the chances looked bleak. At the same time, I was open to divine intervention and willing to show up and do the work to make the impossible possible. This was the same mindset that Alan Christianson had used to combat his illness, and he used what he learned in the process to help others. It was the Miracle Mindset.

The first element of the Miracle Mindset was to view each challenge in life as an opportunity to step up, develop new skills, and become a better person. I longed yet again for Grant to see that the accident had been a gift. It was his fresh start.

"Don't wish it was easier," I told Grant as we walked out toward the car together. "Make yourself stronger."

Warrior Mom's Mantra

Listen to your instincts—they're the most powerful tool we have as moms! Pay attention to that little voice telling you to step up and make a difference. And don't worry about how tough it might be, either. Past challenges have already taught you all the strength and patience you need.

9

You Can't Course-Correct Standing Still

Only a few weeks after he came home full-time, Grant decided that he wanted to go back to school. I knew he was lonely and bored at home, but for once I was the one saying, "He's not ready." Grant was doing great physically, but cognitively he still had a long way to go. He still got overstimulated just hanging out with Bryce and his friends. How would he make it through the day at the busy, hectic high school?

I had my doubts, but once again it was clear that whatever would make Grant happy was the best thing for him. It made sense that he wanted to go to school—that's where sixteen-year-old boys were during the day. Without being there, Grant was completely isolated. Marcey had told John and me many times that Grant would benefit from a regular structure and routine, but with no school to go to, this was difficult to accomplish. Maybe having a reason to get up in the morning and get out the door would be good for him even if it was challenging. Maybe a new challenge would help make him stronger.

John and I set up a meeting at Grant's old high school. Grant wanted to go back to his original classes and continue his junior year, but we all knew this was impossible. There was no way he'd be able to keep up. When the principal suggested that Grant join the special education class, I initially bristled at the idea. Most of the kids in that class were on the autism spectrum. Some others were physically disabled. Grant was neither, but there was no other option. He didn't fit in anywhere.

On Grant's first day back at school, I braced myself for what I assumed was the inevitable—an outburst that would get Grant kicked out of school. This was a familiar feeling. When Grant was younger, I spent many school days nervously staring at my phone, waiting for a call from his teacher saying that Grant had an outburst and needed to be taken home. This time I spent most of the day on the phone doing question-and-answer sessions with followers of the Virgin Diet, and I was shocked when my personal line didn't ring all day. Grant came home right on time, smiling proudly, and I was amazed.

Grant continued to do well for his first few weeks back at school. Marcey had been right about the structure. Grant got himself up and out the door to school more enthusiastically than he ever had before the accident. He quickly became the unofficial teacher's helper in his class. By then he was functioning at a higher level than most of the other kids in the class, and playing the role of helper gave him a huge boost in confidence.

After school one day, I took Grant to see Dr. Daniel Amen to get a SPECT scan of his brain. A SPECT scan is a nuclear imaging test that shows how certain organs are functioning. Fortunately for us, Grant had already been a patient of Dr. Amen's before the accident. I had taken Grant to him after reading Dr. Amen's book *Healing ADD* back when some of Grant's doctors thought he might have attention deficit disorder instead of bipolar disorder. This meant that Dr. Amen had preaccident scans of Grant's brain to compare to his new scans, which was enormously helpful.

Grant's new scans showed a "toxic brain" and very low blood flow to the cerebellum. This explained Grant's persistent issues with language and focus. The cerebellum is in charge of coordination, language, and the ability to quickly integrate new information. It was amazing to see the damage to Grant's brain so clearly in the images. While I already knew that Grant's anger and explosive behavior were not his fault, actually seeing the cause of those issues drove this fact home in a whole new way.

After he finished examining Grant's scans, Dr. Amen called us into his office.

"Grant, it's time for you to take up a new sport," Dr. Amen said with a smile. I hesitated, waiting to hear what Grant would say. He was already working out with a trainer three times a week and getting close to being in even better physical shape than he was before the accident. Grant didn't need a new sport; he needed help with his cognition. I was relieved when Dr. Amen continued, "Have you ever played table tennis?"

Grant stared back at him blankly, as if he didn't understand. I realized that he didn't recognize that name. "Ping-Pong!" I said, jumping in before Grant could get frustrated. "Grant loves Ping-Pong."

"Good," Dr. Amen said. "I want you to play it as much as you can." He turned to look at me. "One of the recommendations I typically make when I see low cerebellum activity is coordination exercises," he explained. "My favorite is table tennis, because you've got to get your eyes, your hands, and your feet to all work together at the same time while you think about your spin on the balls. It's a quick-reaction sport."

We went out that night and bought a Ping-Pong table. There was no free space in the house big enough to accommodate it, so we moved the dining room table into the garage and replaced it with the Ping-Pong table. I figured it could double as a dining table for the time being.

Grant took to Ping-Pong right away, even though he was very slow and almost never hit the ball at first. He swung wildly at the ball, often missing it by several inches. But his improvement was fast and dramatic, and as he improved, he wanted to play more and more. After John, Bryce, and I all got completely sick of playing, we put up one side of the table so Grant could play by himself, hitting balls against the back wall.

The more Grant played, the better he got, and I could see how his improved speed and agility translated into clearer speech and easier access to the information in his brain. This, in combination with Grant's work with Marcey, led to huge improvements in a short amount of time. He didn't struggle as much to find the right words, and his sentences became more linear and straightforward. The better Grant was able to communicate, the more confident he grew, and as a result, the frequency of his outbursts decreased even more. It was amazing to see how much something as simple as Ping-Pong could change his entire outlook.

When I wasn't with Grant, I was working with readers who were following the Virgin Diet. I was happy that so many people were benefiting from the book. It seemed like all the hard work I'd done while sitting next to Grant's hospital bed was worth it. While leading question-and-answer sessions with readers, I got a ton of helpful feedback, and I quickly noticed a common theme—sugar. I realized that many people had an even more complicated relationship to sugar than I'd originally thought.

I got to work creating a framework to look at sugar in a whole new way. When I told my agent about the new framework, she told me, "Well, that has to be your next book."

At first I wasn't sure. On the one hand, it felt too soon to be thinking about another book. I was still in the throes of supporting the first launch. But with the success of *The Virgin Diet* and Grant's recovery, it made sense to make the most of this opportunity.

As I began a trial of my new program, I realized how imperfect the Virgin Diet was to begin with. It was helping tens of thousands of people lose weight, but maybe the impact could have been even greater if I had included more about sugar from the very beginning.

There was no time to look backward, though. I had to move forward based on what was happening in that moment, and the feedback on the new program was clear—it worked. My agent and I quickly put together a proposal for the new book based on the results of the trial program. When she sold it, I was flooded with relief. For the first time since the night of Grant's accident I thought, *Maybe everything really is going to be okay.* Not only had I sold another book, but Grant was also doing well back at school, and Bryce was thriving. It felt like everything was finally starting to settle down, and we were beginning to come out on the other side of this.

As I signed the contracts for the new book deal, it struck me that maybe it was for the best that I hadn't delved deeper into sugar in *The Virgin Diet*—not simply so that I could sell another book, but because this gave me another chance to help even more people. No program could ever be 100 percent perfect, and if I'd waited for mine to be, I would have been waiting forever. I could have viewed it as a setback or seen the Virgin Diet as incomplete. But by pushing forward, starting with an imperfect program and adjusting course along the way, I'd ended up with a bestseller, a new book deal, and thousands of success stories. I couldn't have planned it better even if I'd actually planned it better.

I realized that I had been able to focus on one program at a time and ultimately help even more people than I had ever hoped to by being present in each moment and facing the challenges and setbacks as they came. I never would have come up with a new framework for the Sugar Impact Diet if I'd been stuck on the idea that I'd messed up by not including more about sugar in *The Virgin Diet*. There was nothing I could do about that now except to move forward accordingly. So that's what I did.

This reminded me of the night of Grant's accident when I stepped outside to clear my head. I remember smelling the mixture of exhaust from emergency vehicles and pollen from a nearby bed of flowering plants. I felt the dryness of the Southern California air. As I focused on these sensations, I finally realized how important it was to be fully present.

This continued throughout Grant's recovery. Every decision was vital to Grant's future and well-being, but it was paralyzing to think of all the consequences of what I was doing. In the midst of the chaos, I had to remind myself to be fully present in each moment. I was angry with Grant that night and terrified of what the rest of his life might look like, but I had to let go of my anger, fear, and resentment in order to make decisions that would move us in the right direction.

Being fully present taught me to be flexible, which was crucial in order to ride the twists and turns of Grant's recovery. This is true when facing any sort of challenge. Problems are seldom straightforward and often require flexibility. Forcing myself into the present clarified my goals, even when they kept changing. I was forced to stop thinking about the past or the future and had to focus all of my attention on the decisions at hand. I knew there would be setbacks, but I was open and ready for them.

I had to constantly scrap plans I had been fully committed to just moments before, whether it was moving Grant to Children's

Hospital when we saw how frustrated he was being limited to the hospital bed, dealing with his outbursts, starting therapy even when he couldn't bear any weight on his lower body, or ultimately bringing him home from the hospital far sooner than his doctors advised. With no idea what was going to happen from one day—indeed, often from one moment—to the next, all of these decisions had to be made based on whatever information I had at the time.

None of them were perfect. That much was clear. Grant had a pseudoaneurysm that delayed his transfer to Children's Hospital (and could have killed him); his outbursts left John scratched and bruised; Grant was frustrated being limited to a wheelchair in therapy; and bringing him home when we did had forced me to wrestle pills out of his hands and call the police on my own son.

At the same time, it was clear to me that each of these decisions and every setback had also led us forward, however imperfectly. Where would Grant be now if we hadn't taken each one of those steps? There was no way for us to have made better or more well-informed decisions. The only other option was to stand still and do nothing. While Grant's survival and recovery were on the line, I didn't consider that an option at all.

It turned out that one of the best things we did for Grant throughout his entire recovery was to start him on therapy as early as we did. When we first got to Children's Hospital, the therapists had to be incredibly creative to find ways to work with Grant despite his limitations. His heel was still in a cast, and his temper frequently flared. It would have been easy to put off therapy until his cast came off and he could focus for more than five minutes at a time. But we didn't know if or when that would happen, so we had to start where we were at that moment.

The unpredictable nature of Grant's injury continuously forced us to be present. We had no way of knowing what state he'd be in tomorrow. We could either work with what we had at that moment or risk losing that opportunity completely. It turned out that Grant was in the perfect position to start his therapy. We didn't have to wait until he had fewer outbursts, because as his confidence in his abilities grew, the outbursts naturally decreased in frequency. We didn't have to wait for his cast to come off, and when it did, he already had a head start.

It was difficult to let go of my fear and anger when making each decision, but I saw now how crucial my presence had been at each moment. Grant's outcome would have been very different if I had faced every obstacle while thinking *I can't believe Grant got hit by a car* or *What if he's paralyzed for the rest of his life?*

As was true of *The Virgin Diet*, looking backward and questioning my decisions would get me nowhere. So would looking forward with doubt and fear. The only way to move forward through any challenge was to use the information I had in each moment as an opportunity to make a positive impact on the future.

Grant had been back at school for almost two months when he asked to join the regular physical education class. This made sense to me. He was in great shape, and there was no reason for him to be in gym class with the kids from special education.

I was working from home the first day Grant tried this new arrangement, and I could tell that it hadn't gone well before he even made it into the house. He shuffled up the driveway with his head down and his hands stuffed into his pockets. "I hate everyone!" he shouted as soon as he got inside. The front door slammed so hard that the whole house shook.

"Honey," I said calmly, following him toward his room, "what happened?" I should have known better than to ask any questions when he was in this state. He immediately shut the door to his room and stayed in there, refusing to go to school the next morning or the one after that.

It took days of gentle prodding for me to find out that a boy in his new gym class had told Grant, "You didn't really get in an accident; you're just stupid."

This just about broke me. No parent wants to see her kid hurt. I had already seen mine physically torn apart, millimeters away from death. But witnessing his emotional pain was somehow even harder.

After that, Grant decided that he didn't like people, period. He flat-out refused to go back to school. John and I agreed to just let him be for the moment and try re-enrolling him in the fall, but Grant was restless at home. His knee had fully healed and he was running sprints, but his cognitive improvement had slowed.

Grant was frustrated that he wasn't progressing. He desperately wanted to move forward, but once again, he couldn't seem to stop holding himself back. We signed him up for a few classes at the local community college, but right away he made excuses not to go. While Bryce expressed his dismay at Grant's self-defeating behavior, it was obvious to me that he was afraid of being hurt again.

Thankfully, Grant wasn't having as many outbursts, but he wasn't doing much of anything else, either. He played video games and Ping-Pong, he argued with Bryce, and he argued with me. "Grant," I said, turning off the video game he was playing, "you've got to do something."

"I'm not going," he told me yet again. "I hate people. What's the point?"

"You don't have to go back to school," I told him, "but you have to do something."

"Like what?" he asked.

For once, I was at a complete loss for how to answer. It felt like Grant's life had completely derailed. I too constantly asked myself what the rest of his life would be like, but I knew how important it was to focus on the moment and tune out my fear about what the future might hold. I took a breath and forced myself to be present, as I had done that first night at the hospital. I understood how disappointed Grant was that returning to school hadn't worked out the way he'd planned. But I also realized that he had to let go of that disappointment and hurt in order to move forward. We both did.

"Grant," I said, struggling to find the words to tell him what I'd learned, "forget about what's happened in the past and try to envision a way forward. You can't course-correct standing still."

Finally we managed to move forward by hiring a private teacher to work with Grant at home in addition to the physical therapist we already had on board. But Marcey was still the most important member of our team. As he continued to work with Marcey, Grant's writing started to come along, as well as his receptive language. Now when Marcey showed Grant two cards with a word written on each of them and asked, "Which one says 'apple'?" Grant could point to the right one.

As he got better at expressing himself, Grant's outbursts came less and less frequently. He stopped taking pills and trying to run away from home. Now he could put words to his feelings and tell Marcey that he was angry because he had no control over his own life and virtually no independence. Even though he was no longer in school, he needed some sort of structure. When Marcey told John and me about that, we worked together to create a daily calendar so Grant could have more autonomy and know what to expect from one day to the next.

Marcey knew how important it was to boost Grant's self-esteem, so she spent a lot of her time working with him on social skills—staying on topic, taking turns in a conversation, and not interrupting. When I took the boys out to dinner soon afterward, I saw what a difference this was making. For the first time in as long as I could remember, Grant waited for Bryce to finish talking about his day before jumping in to talk about himself.

For a while, working at home with a private tutor seemed to be the answer we had been searching for. The tutor was able to tailor his lesson to whatever Grant was interested in, which seemed to change from one day to the next. One day Grant decided that he wanted to become a computer programmer, so his teacher created a lesson about binary code. Grant was excited at first, but then quickly lost interest. After a few more false starts, Grant gradually stopped cooperating and completing his assignments. When I got on his case about it, his response was "What's the point?" He just didn't have the motivation.

When we returned to Dr. Amen for a follow-up visit, we saw that the blood flow to Grant's cerebellum had improved by 30 percent since the last scan. This visual proof that we were moving forward, however imperfectly, sustained me through the doubts and difficult moments that kept coming. I was feeling anxious about where Grant was headed. What if we never found a way to get him back to school? The regular high school wasn't going to work. The night classes at the local community college didn't work. Even the tutor didn't seem to be working.

All of this jumping around from one thing to the next left me feeling stressed and antsy. Grant's outbursts had diminished, but they still happened, and when they did, I wondered if this was a side effect of the traumatic brain injury, a symptom of his bipolar disorder, or just Grant being Grant. How would I ever be able to distinguish one from the other?

"I just want to get him settled," I confessed to Marcey when I picked Grant up from a speech therapy appointment soon after. I hadn't sat in on one of his sessions in a while, and I made a point to go that day to see if he was showing any signs of progression. I was desperate for any proof that he was moving forward.

"Let me show you something," Marcey said, gesturing for me to follow her into the treatment room. I walked in and sat down on the couch. "Grant, let's show your mom what you can do," she told him with a supportive smile.

Grant sat in a chair holding a book and looking nervous. I looked at the book, which he had opened to the last page. It was one that I had read to him and Bryce all the time when they were little. I figured that Marcey had been reading it to him in therapy. Grant could now recognize all the letters and their sounds, but he still wasn't reading. Or so I thought.

"Puff, puff, chug, chug. Up the mountain went the Little Blue Engine," Grant read in a slow, halting voice. "And all the time she kept saying, 'I think I can, I think I can.'" I looked at Marcey in amazement. She caught my eye from across the room and winked at me.

"Up, up, up, the Little Blue Engine climbed. At last she reached the top of the mountain. Down below lay the city." Grant finally looked up at me. His smile was contagious, and I smiled back. "'Hurray, hurray,' cried the dolls and animals. 'The boys and girls will be so happy,' said the toy clown. 'All because you helped us, Little Blue Engine.'"

I reached into my purse for a tissue and swiped at my eyes. "The Little Blue Engine just smiled. But as she puffed down the mountain, she seemed to say, 'I thought I could . . . I thought I could . . . I thought I could.'"

Watching Grant, I could practically see his self-esteem going up as he read. His voice grew stronger and more confident with each line of text. As I listened, I realized that over the past few weeks, I hadn't been doing a good job of being fully present. After Grant stopped going to school, I had continued taking steps forward, but I'd done so while holding on to the idea of him returning to school one day. It was time to let go of that idea completely in order to clear the path in front of us.

When we were in the hospital and I first set the goal for Grant to recover at 110 percent, I didn't have a specific idea in mind of what that would look like. I just knew that it was a fresh start. But it couldn't really be fresh if I was still attached to the goals I had for Grant before the accident—finishing school, going to college, and so on. I had to take my own advice and stop looking backward. If I was going to be open to whatever life had in store, that meant being open to recalibrating the goals I had previously taken for granted. I had to embrace the setbacks that were part of the journey. We needed to start where Grant was now, not where he was before the accident, when he was in the hospital, or even the day before.

This, I realized, was the second piece of the Miracle Mindset—making decisions based on the facts available at each moment, with the willingness to change course if needed. Maybe Grant would never graduate from high school, but now I asked myself, *What if that doesn't matter at all?* After everything Grant had been through, it was more important for him to be healthy and happy than it was for him to hit typical teenage milestones. Perhaps graduating from high school wasn't relevant to Grant's true purpose on this planet. Maybe there was something bigger out there for him.

Watching Grant close the book with a proud smile on his face,

I vowed to completely let go of my own expectations and fears so I could help him move forward. Like the Little Blue Engine, Grant stood now at the top of the mountain. The path from here on was uncertain—and likely full of setbacks. Our only hope of seeing it clearly was to be present in the moment without any fears, doubts, and worries clouding our vision. This was how Grant would ultimately forge his own course.

WARRIOR MOM'S MANTRA

As mothers, we all want the best for our families. But if you're waiting for perfection, you're in for a long wait! It's our job to stay present and look for answers to today's challenges, instead of being paralyzed by past worries or anger. (Remember that Little Blue Engine . . .)

10

Your Limitations Will Become Your Life

In early May, I met with my executive director, Susan Tafralis, to plan our business strategy for the next quarter. Susan's title had changed over the years, but the best way to describe our relationship is that she is like my older sister. She had been working for me for seventeen years in various capacities, but always as my right-hand woman. In that time, she'd become more like a family member than an employee.

When Grant and Bryce were little, Susan often helped by dropping them off and picking them up from school. She gave them special treats, and held Grant lovingly when he had an outburst. To them, she was Auntie Susan, and to me she was a rock. When I trusted the wrong person years before and got cheated out of so much money that I ended up nearly bankrupt, Susan stepped in with a loan that consisted of her entire life savings—about $50,000. When I refused the loan, Susan insisted, simply transferring the money into our business account without my permission or knowledge.

Before getting down to business, I asked Susan, "How is your mother?" Susan's ninety-year-old mother had entered the hospital with dementia and some other health issues right around the same time Grant had his accident. For the past several months, Susan had been working by her mother's bedside. When Grant was still in the hospital, we often joked that we were living parallel lives, but of course unlike Grant, Susan's mother would most likely stay in the hospital for the rest of her life.

"More or less the same," Susan told me, "but some things have changed that I want to tell you about."

As I listened, I noticed Susan's smile and the warm glow to her cheeks. The last few times I'd seen her, I was worried about whether or not she was taking care of herself. But now she seemed so full of energy and hope. "Remember how I told you about the awful food in the hospital?" she asked me.

"Yes," I told her, "and I told you to insist on something better for your mom or just bring your own food. No one should have to eat that garbage."

Susan nodded. "Well, I finally did," she said. "I didn't think I had any power to change what was going on in the hospital," she continued, "but when I heard about everything you did for Grant, I realized that I could fight to make things better for my mom. I started fighting for every meal she ate, and then I fought for them to change her diaper more quickly when she soiled herself, and guess what?"

"What?" I hoped Susan got a good response, or else I would have been responsible for getting her mother kicked out of the hospital.

"They listened!" Susan sounded like she couldn't believe it herself. "They actually listened to me, and we've completely changed the quality of care that my mother is getting. JJ," she continued, reaching for my hand, "it's all because you gave me the courage. You gave me the strength. You showed me that just because a doctor says something, that doesn't make it so.

"It's not just doctors and hospitals," Susan continued. "You've made me feel more confident in other situations, too. Just the other day I went out to dinner and the waiter brought me the wrong meal. Normally I would have just accepted it, but then I thought, *Why shouldn't I get the meal that I ordered?* It may sound silly, but it's really changed my life."

"It doesn't sound silly at all," I told her. I never used to stand up for myself either, even when it came to small things, and I knew how big a difference even something as minor as this could make.

"You'll be happy to hear I've been better about my diet too," Susan said, nodding her head. "It's as if I finally feel worthy of the things I most want."

We shifted our conversation to business soon after, but I couldn't stop thinking about what Susan had said. Was it possible that I had given her strength and boosted her self-worth just by doing what came naturally and advocating for Grant?

While I was meeting with Susan, John had taken Grant to a

follow-up appointment at the audiologist. When we had left Children's Hospital for the last time in January, they suddenly mentioned that Grant was having problems hearing out of his right ear. This was new information. Among the many, many health concerns that had been raised during Grant's four months in the hospital, his hearing was never among them. All of a sudden, we had to find an audiologist and figure out what was going on with Grant's ears.

At the first appointment with the audiologist back in January, it had been impossible to tell why Grant wasn't hearing. He failed the hearing test, but we didn't know if it was because there was something wrong with Grant's ear or if it was a result of the traumatic brain injury. Now that the latest SPECT scan showed such a vast improvement in Grant's brain, we wanted to get his hearing checked again to see if that had also improved.

It hadn't.

When John and Grant got home from the audiologist, Grant went right to his room to play video games. I looked at John, my eyebrows raised, waiting for the verdict. "Grant has complete hearing loss in his right ear," he told me.

"What can we do?" I asked, but John shook his head.

"There's nothing we can do about the hearing itself," he said. "The doctor said the eardrum is picking up vibrations, but it appears the cochlea was damaged by the head trauma. The vibrations aren't stimulating the nerve endings in the cochlea, so there's no chance of recovering the hearing loss in that ear."

John explained that the doctor had given them a referral to get Grant fitted for a hearing aid, and that was that.

I took Grant and Bryce out to dinner that night. As we sat at the table looking at our menus, I kept darting my eyes to my right to look at Grant. He had surprised me by reacting completely calmly to this news instead of throwing either a tantrum or a pity party. Maybe he hadn't understood.

I thought about all the health issues Grant had faced over the last few months—his torn aorta; the thirteen fractures, including a crushed heel and two broken femurs; road rash; brain bleeds; and a massive traumatic brain injury. "Well," I finally said to Grant, "after everything you've overcome, if you had to get stuck with one issue, I'd say that hearing loss in one ear is really no big deal."

Grant didn't say anything, and I suddenly wondered if he could hear me. "Grant?"

This time he shook his head. "That doctor doesn't know what she's talking about," he said. "I've got vibrations. That means I can hear. Why should I listen to what she says, anyway?"

Over the next few weeks, Grant embraced the challenge that his hearing loss presented, becoming fascinated by different sets of headphones that he could adjust to determine how much he heard. He used this to his advantage, tuning us out when he wanted to by turning down the volume on his headset. The doctor had told Grant that he might struggle with balance issues as a result of the hearing loss, so Grant took it upon himself to add balance exercises to his gym workouts. He kept growing stronger.

This was one of the first times since the accident that Grant had been directly told that he wouldn't be able to do something, and I was so proud to see him respond with this determination to prove the doctor wrong. When I thought about Susan using my example to advocate for her mother in the hospital and send food back at a restaurant, I realized that this was no accident. Both of them had described their new attitudes in such similar ways, echoing the way John and I had responded to every negative prediction that had been made about Grant since that awful night of the accident.

I realized that maybe Grant wasn't buying into what the audiologist had said because John and I hadn't bought into the doctors' prognoses. They said that Grant wouldn't survive the airlift or the heart surgery, that he would never wake up, and that he would never walk or function normally ever again, but here he was, standing next to me. It was astonishing to think that our refusal to accept these limiting predictions had not only saved Grant's life but continued to help him recover more and more each day.

This made me feel so grateful that I'd done the work earlier in my life to rid myself of the limiting beliefs instilled in me when I was a girl.

I was born an entrepreneur, but it took many years for me to figure out what that meant. In part I think this was because I was so different from everyone in the super-traditional family I was adopted into. My mother was a housewife who reminded me of June Cleaver, and my father was the typical breadwinner who worked for the same company for forty years, waiting for his ship to come in.

Even as a young child, this seemed backward to me. I was motivated to get out there and create opportunities for myself instead of waiting for them to arrive at my doorstep. When I was five, I roamed the neighborhood after school with a list of my services. "I can walk your dog. I can cut your grass," it read in my semilegible kindergarten handwriting.

When I was twelve years old, my family went on vacation for a week to Lake Tahoe. I saw this free week as a great opportunity to get a lot of things done, and I packed my record player, my sewing machine, my tap shoes, and my list of goals for the week. I was eagerly unpacking in our vacation house when my mom came into the room and sat down next to me on the bed. She picked up my list of goals. "Practice tap," it read. "Sew a new top for school." My mom put down the list, covered her face with her hands, and started to cry.

"What's wrong, Mom?" I was scared that something horrible had happened, or maybe I had done something to upset her.

She shook her head. "I just want you to relax and be happy," she told me, smoothing my hair away from my forehead. I frowned. I knew my mother loved me, but even then I was aware that relaxing didn't equal happy for me. In order to be happy, I needed to be accomplishing or creating something.

It was hard to embrace my entrepreneurial spirit when just being myself seemed to upset my mother so much. She always told me to "just fit in" and "follow the rules," and in my efforts to make her happy, I did my best to listen to her. I hid the things that were special and unique about me and tried to fit in. But it was a struggle. My mom's voice was always fighting my inner voice that told me to shatter the rules and make up my own. "Don't study so hard," she said, and when I stayed up all night working on a project anyway, she'd tell me, "You're like the Little Engine That Could!"

As I grew to be six feet tall, my mom told me to never wear high heels, not to be too loud, not to be so bold, and not to stand so tall. Over the years, I literally started shrinking. I played small, I didn't go after my dreams, and eventually I started wondering how many opportunities I was missing out on.

Every parent wants to protect his or her child, and I knew that was exactly what my mother was trying to do for me. She didn't want me to go after things that she thought were unrealistic and end up getting hurt. But in the process, she instilled some strong limiting beliefs in me about who I was and what I deserved.

When I started my business, my belief that I didn't deserve what I most wanted in life kept me from growing. I knew deep down that I had more to contribute and my business could be bigger, but I didn't know how to make this happen. When Grant was twelve and Bryce was eleven and I was still barely earning enough to make ends meet, I had finally had enough. I was determined to push my career to the next level, and I hired a business coach for the first time to help me get there. I was already in debt, I had just lost my only stable source of income due to a contract ending, and my new coach's fee was $100,000. There were plenty of people who thought I was crazy, but I knew I had to do this.

That coach helped me get rid of my debt and create a steady income quickly. But more important, she helped me rid myself of the limiting belief that I wasn't worthy of a life that mattered. This had been holding me back for my entire life, and I wanted to start thinking bigger about my life and my career. I knew I'd never get there if I didn't believe I deserved it. People criticized me for spending money that I couldn't afford, but in my eyes I couldn't afford *not* to learn all the things she taught me.

When we first started working together, I thought the coach was going to give me a straightforward plan to grow my business. I was in for quite a surprise! For months, she taught me nothing about business, or so it seemed. Instead, she coached me on mindset. "Where are the numbers?" I kept asking her. "Show me the numbers."

Instead, the first thing she did was ask me to get out a paper and pen and write down all the things I would want in my life if money, time, and location were no object. "It can literally be anything," she told me. "I want you to really go crazy here and write down your wildest dreams."

I thought for a moment and then wrote that I wanted a Jaguar convertible and a condo in Maui. My coach looked at my list and asked, "Why only one Jaguar?"

I told her, "Well, I just need one."

She smiled at me. "It's not about what you need," she responded. "It's about what you want."

I looked at my list again and realized how much I'd limited myself without even being aware of it. Why had I chosen only a condo in Maui? Why not a house? Why not the whole darn island?

"You'll never outgrow your self-image," my coach told me, and I realized in that moment that I would never get where I wanted to go if I didn't believe that I was worth it. It wasn't the material things like condos or Jaguars that were important—it was the extent of my self-belief. The truth was that my career was exactly where I believed it could be. I would only ever be as successful as I thought I should be, and I had been limiting myself based on my low self-worth.

Instead of believing that I could keep growing, I was acting like a circus elephant who had been trained with a chain around its foot. After a while, it didn't matter whether the chain was still there. I was staying in place by force of habit. It was time to break free of that chain and finally move forward.

My coach told me that the first step was to surround myself with possibility instead of my own limitations. "If you want to start thinking bigger about your own life," she told me, "find other people who've already reached your goals and who believe that you can too. Surround yourself with people who can think bigger than you. It's going to be painful," she continued, "but you're going to look at your friends and realize that some of them have to go."

I bristled at this idea at first, but I took a long, hard look at who I really wanted to be spending time with, and it was the people who were living the type of exciting, risky, entrepreneurial life that I wanted. As I began to seek out and spend more time around these truly successful, abundance-minded people and then went back to see my old friends, it became clear that I still had some people in my life who were holding me back. These people always found a way to subtly put me down and make me feel small. When I excitedly told them about my plans to pursue my wildest dreams, they looked at me as if I was crazy and then tried to talk me out of it.

I knew that these people, including my mother, meant well.

They were either afraid that I would fail or afraid that I would succeed and leave them behind. But at the end of the day, they were operating from a place of fear, and I saw that I needed to be around people who were focused on possibilities instead. These were the ones who were excited for me to rise up and wanted to help me get where I was going.

Of course I couldn't get rid of my mother—nor did I want to—so I worked on creating boundaries. This was why I knew that I couldn't speak to her every day when Grant was in the hospital. I had to protect myself from her fear when I was at my most vulnerable.

Even after making all these changes and the years of success that followed, I still struggled with my self-worth for years. I had deeply internalized the limiting beliefs handed down to me. When I was chosen to appear on a regular basis on *The Dr. Phil Show* as the nutrition expert, I often felt like an impostor. I was constantly afraid of being "found out" for not being good enough. Ultimately, I didn't feel worthy. Who was I to be acting like a big shot on national TV? Each time I drove onto the lot, showed my ID, and walked to my dressing room, I felt like a fraud. Every day I wondered if this would be the day they figured out the truth and told me that I wasn't good enough to be there.

I didn't realize how common this was or that it had a name—impostor syndrome—until one day when I was standing among a group of beautiful, successful women sharing the fact that they all felt this way. It struck me that maybe our fear of being impostors was really indicative of our stretching ourselves, breaking free of our limitations, and liberating ourselves from the chains around our feet.

All the women in that group were entrepreneurs who'd taken big risks in their lives and careers. It made sense, in a way, that we all felt the discomfort of surpassing our self-imposed limits. If we'd all played small and settled for unfulfilling office jobs, there would be no reason for us to feel like impostors. We wouldn't have been challenging anyone's expectations for us, including our own.

From that point on, I began to see my impostor syndrome as a good thing. I realized that every time I took a step forward in my career and had to stop and ask myself if I was good enough to be there, it meant I was pushing myself out to a bigger level. Each time I did this, I had to adjust and get comfortable before I could go on to push out even bigger and expand my comfort zone even more. It was a huge relief to completely let go of the limiting beliefs that were holding me back and finally feel free to embrace my gifts. I learned to value myself and what I had to offer, and ultimately I realized that I could never be an impostor if I was doing the work that I was put on this planet to do.

It wasn't until I spoke to Susan and saw the way Grant reacted to his hearing loss that I realized the full impact of getting rid of my limiting beliefs. This hadn't just helped me move forward in my career; it had also helped me save my son. This was the third component of the Miracle Mindset: surpassing self-imposed limitations and believing that I deserved everything in life that I wanted.

How would things have played out differently in the aftermath of Grant's accident if I had never done the work to rid myself of the voices in my head that told me I wasn't worthy? I'll never know for sure. If I had still been listening to those voices, maybe I would also have listened to the doctor's initial prognosis that Grant wasn't going to make it through the first night. Perhaps I wouldn't have fought to have him airlifted or even sought out other options to begin with. Maybe I would have listened when they said that Grant would never wake up and wouldn't have bothered with the progesterone cream, essential oils, or fish oil. I might have assumed the doctors were right when they said he would never walk again and have left him in the hospital bed to stagnate instead of starting him on therapy as soon as possible. I would have given up on my son.

Instead, by the night of Grant's accident, I was done letting people—including myself—limit me. There was no way I was going to give in to my own fear or listen to anyone's negativity and settle for the prognosis the doctors offered or the statistics they'd thrown at us. For Grant, I wasn't going to settle for anything less than greatness. He wasn't going to live or die just because a doctor said he would, and I wouldn't let anyone hold him back. Instead, I surrounded him at every moment with possibility and hope. Instead of focusing on the 99.98 percent chance that Grant was going to die, I thought only about the .02 percent chance that he would live.

Now that Grant was reading, his interest in working with his tutor had returned. He voraciously read book after book about whatever subject interested him in the moment. First it was psychology. He inhaled the entire works of Sigmund Freud. Then it was the lives of great artists. He read biography after biography and worked to duplicate their paintings. When I saw the beautiful and skillful work he was doing, I was so grateful that I had stopped limiting him by trying to get him back to school. The work he was doing now was more important and truer to his purpose than anything he would have learned in high school.

When he wasn't reading or drawing, Grant was in the gym or playing tennis with John. With all the balance exercises he was doing and the Ping-Pong he was playing, I expected Grant to be getting pretty good, but when I saw him competing against John that spring, I was amazed. Grant was strong, fast, and precise. He gave John, who'd been teaching tennis lessons for decades, a run for his money.

"How did you get so good?" I asked Grant afterward.

"I've been working on my eyes," he said. At first I wasn't sure what Grant meant. Then he reached his arms out to his sides and showed me the exercises he'd been doing to improve his peripheral vision. "If I can't hear, then I want to see better," he told me with a grin.

"I'm so proud of you," I told him. Not only had Grant refused to believe the audiologist's negative predictions, but he'd also used them as motivation to make himself better.

Although he had responded so well to the hearing loss, there were still plenty of times when his lack of independence and inability to do simple things left him frustrated and angry. Just a few days later, Grant wanted to walk back to the tennis courts by himself to practice. It wasn't far from our house, but I wasn't ready to let Grant walk anywhere alone yet. Grant often wanted to be outside by himself and go for a walk. It sounded so simple. But after the accident, the incidents with the pills, and his attempts to walk himself back to the hospital, I felt it just wasn't safe.

At the same time, all of Grant's friends were learning to drive. We saw them sometimes on the road or in the parking lots of our local stores, showing off in their new cars. Every time I saw one of them, I couldn't help but think that Grant should have been reaching that milestone too. Instead, he was dependent on John or me to drive him around, like a child. He couldn't even go on a walk by himself.

"There's nothing I can do," Grant complained when I wouldn't let him walk to the tennis courts. "I shouldn't even be alive." It was quite a leap from taking a walk to his purpose on this planet, but that's what it was like with Grant. It was hard for me to keep up sometimes.

Before Grant's accident, I never realized how important it could be for a sixteen-year-old to have a life purpose. After coming face-to-face with death, Grant seemed to realize that he had come back to do more than just sit around and play video games. He sensed that there was something bigger that he was meant to be doing here, and his frustration stemmed from not knowing what or how.

I desperately wanted Grant to think big for himself. I too believed that he had survived for a reason, and I was determined to help him discover what that was instead of letting him be held back by the things he couldn't do.

"Let's look at what you can do instead of what you can't," I said to Grant. "Your limitations will become your life." I grabbed a pen and a piece of paper and sat down on the couch next to him. "Let's come from a place of possibilities instead, and list them out."

As we sat there and listed out all of the things Grant could do—read, draw, play tennis, go to the gym, etc.—I could see his confidence return. He might not have been able to drive or even take a walk by himself, but he could certainly do a lot more than any of his doctors had ever thought he would. And I knew that if he continued to believe he was worthy, he'd keep doing more and more.

"You inspire so many people just by being," I told him. "You inspire me." He looked up from our list with a smile that was, just like him, limitless.

Warrior Mom's Mantra
One moment we're protecting our newborns, the next we're helping them stand, then take their first steps—and that process never ends. When moms live in a place of possibilities rather than fear, we can show our children how to keep growing and moving forward.

11

Little Hinges Swing Big Doors

Ever since Grant had gotten home from the hospital, I'd been longing to take him and Bryce on a vacation. After everything we'd been through over the past several months, I wanted the three of us to get away for a few days and just be together. No hospitals. No doctors. No therapy. No work. Just my boys and me, relaxing and having fun.

Of course I had to wait until Grant was stable enough to go a few days without receiving any medical care and (hopefully) without having an outburst. By the time Bryce's school year ended, I felt that Grant was ready. July would be the perfect time for our trip. Bryce was done with school, Grant was medically stable and his outbursts had diminished, and for the first time since Grant's accident, I finally felt that I could take some time away from work. *The Virgin*

Diet had finally ended its run on the *New York Times* bestseller list in June after an amazing twenty-six weeks. For the rest of the summer I'd be busy writing *JJ Virgin's Sugar Impact Diet* and hosting my second Mindshare Summit in August. First, it was time to get away.

I had the dates for the trip set, but I couldn't figure out where we should go. Grant was resistant to the very idea of a vacation. He wanted to stay at home where he was comfortable. Bryce, on the other hand, was always ready for an adventure. How could I find something that would be fun for both of them? To make matters even more complicated, when I mentioned the trip to my mother, she told me that she wanted to come with us. Now I had to cater to an eighty-three-year-old grandmother in addition to a daring fifteen-year-old and a sixteen-year-old with a brain injury.

Finally, I settled on a trip to the Hawaiian island of Kauai. It was a relatively short direct flight away and there seemed to be a variety of activities available there for all of us—beautiful beaches, boat rides, canyons, kayaking, hiking, and so on. I threw myself completely into planning the trip. I wanted everything to be perfect so we could really enjoy this time together, and I created daily itineraries that were filled with activities I hoped all of us would appreciate.

For the first day or two, everything went smoothly. The island was stunningly beautiful. Every view I looked at was more awe-inspiring than the next—the clear turquoise water surrounded by mountain peaks, the rivers branching out in all directions, and the cascading waterfalls. One of the first things we all did together was go on a helicopter ride that revealed views of the island's interior that were even more impressive than anything we'd already seen. We got a bird's-eye view of lush tropical rain forests and the magnificent Waimea Canyon, a fourteen-mile-long geological wonder that our guide told us had been nicknamed the Grand Canyon of the Pacific.

I tore my eyes away from the view for a moment to look at Grant as he took it all in. His forehead was pressed against the glass, his mouth slack in wonder. This was an even more beautiful view to me than anything beyond the helicopter window.

The four of us went out to dinner that night, and I saw yet again how much Grant's work with Marcey was helping him develop his social skills. He and Bryce were sitting next to each other, deep in conversation. I wished I could hear what they were saying, but I knew better than to ask. I just watched them talking from across the table until Grant said something that made Bryce laugh. Soon they were both doubled over in hysterics.

As I watched them, I thought about the family vacations we took when the boys were little. Being off of his schedule always threw Grant, and he ended up having a tantrum wherever we went. Bryce reacted by getting angry and withdrawing from the rest of us, while John and I blamed each other. Things were so different now. Despite everything it had taken for us to get here, I was grateful to see how far we'd come.

As so often happened, just the next morning I felt like we were back at square one. I had planned for us to go on a boat trip to see parts of the island that were accessible only by water. Bryce was excited, but Grant didn't want to go. He wanted to stay back at the condo I had rented and play video games on his laptop.

For the next couple of days, I went off on adventure after adventure with Bryce—boat rides, swimming, and zip-lining—while Grant and my mom stayed back at the condo. The only time we were all together was when we went out to eat. Grant loved going out to nice restaurants and we all enjoyed our meals together, but I was so frustrated that I couldn't really appreciate any of it. I had planned this trip so specifically to make everyone happy, and it wasn't going the way I'd imagined. What was the point of being on this amazing island if Grant was going to miss the whole thing by staying indoors?

After struggling for a few days to force everyone to have fun, I decided to take some time to be alone. I went back to Waimea Canyon for a closer look. The view of the interior of the canyon was even more spectacular than the one we'd seen from the helicopter. From where I stood on the lookout, I could see every crag and gorge. It looked like the mountain had been carved away with absolute precision to reveal its true beauty—the red rock that swirled inward as it worked its way down toward the earth and layered itself perfectly over countless shades of green and earthy brown. It was as if a master artist had intentionally sculpted every inch of the canyon to maximize its natural beauty.

But of course I knew it wasn't created that way at all. The canyon's beauty hadn't appeared all at once. It had taken hundreds of years of erosion and untold rivers wearing away at the land bit by bit over time to sculpt it so majestically.

Staring out at the canyon stretching for miles in front of me, I thought about Grant. The cumulative way all the beauty before me had been created was similar to the way Grant had come out of the coma and begun working his way toward recovery. When Grant was in the coma, I had no idea how gradual his awakening would be. I imagined that he would just wake up one day and that would be that. He'd look me in the eye, say, "Hi, Mom," and we'd head off into the sunset—or at least toward the hospital exit.

I should have known better. Whether it's in geology, weight loss, business, or health, big changes don't occur suddenly. They happen in the accumulation of small shifts that add up as a transformation takes place. As winter slowly thaws, spring comes in a beautiful unfolding, not all at once. First the ice and snow melts, then a tiny bud appears, and little by little it finally fully blooms. This canyon hadn't been created in one fell swoop, and it wouldn't have been as impressive if it had. Its true beauty came from the millions of tiny, imperceptible changes that had accrued over the years.

Similarly, Grant didn't come out of the coma in the sudden way I had expected him to. Instead of becoming fully awake all at once, he woke incrementally. From one day to the next, the changes in him were so subtle that it took all my focus and attention to even notice them. When I did, each shift seemed miraculous. Every time he squeezed my hand, wiggled his toes, or fluttered his eyelashes, I was filled with hope.

Throughout that entire process, it would have been so easy for me to focus on everything that was going wrong. New obstacles were constantly presenting themselves, and the positive changes were so gradual that it would have been easy to overlook them. I didn't even notice some of the things that were going well for Grant until Dr. Meyer pointed them out to me. But once she did, my newfound awareness gave me the strength to keep pushing forward.

If before the accident you had told me that I would ever be in the hospital with my comatose son celebrating a finger squeeze with my whole heart, I wouldn't have believed you. That was not really where I wanted to be. But by focusing on the good things that were happening, however small they were, I was able to appreciate each day as it came and accept my new reality.

As I continued to study the canyon, I realized that I had been able to stay positive in the hospital because I'd been focusing on each small step forward rather than letting myself get overwhelmed by the big goal. I had been clear from the beginning on my vision to help Grant get to 110 percent, but trying to get him from a coma to 110 percent all at once would have been overwhelming. It would have paralyzed me. So I set my course in that direction and took small actions each day to get me one step closer to that goal. The size of those steps didn't matter. The important thing was that I was heading in the right direction.

Once the big things were taken care of—fixing Grant's heart, getting his brain oxygenated, and setting his femurs and his heel—I then took whatever small steps I could: getting Grant proper nutrition, using essential oils, throwing balls to him, giving him lollipops, and so on. These small efforts accumulated, leading to big changes, and before I knew it, Grant was responding, looking me in the eye, and then demanding, "Let's go." It started by taking one small step every day to get him further on his path to 110 percent recovery.

Each night when I got back to my hotel room after being in the hospital with Grant all day, I asked myself two questions: *What went well today?* and *What else can I do?* Thinking about what had gone well forced me to look back and take note of every good sign. It was a way of celebrating each small win, however tiny or imperceptible it may have been. There were plenty of days when it seemed like everything was going wrong. But if I looked hard enough, I could always find something to celebrate, even if it was simply the fact that Grant was still alive.

This kept me in a constant state of gratitude and positivity that inspired me to continue trying new things. I'll never know for sure how much each of those smoothies I fed Grant helped him heal, if the oils were helping, or if the progesterone cream was really making a difference, but the sense that I was doing *something* was hugely empowering. On the darkest days, it was helpful to be able to look toward the future, even if that future was just the next hour or the next day.

It was terrifying to watch Grant move his arm back and forth across his torso for hours and hours and later to see him having fits and even hurting himself and others. Asking myself what I could do tomorrow helped me realize that tomorrow might be different from today. Even picturing tomorrow as being a small fraction better was enough to give me hope.

I knew that if Grant simply made it through the night, we'd have a chance to try again tomorrow. That in and of itself was something to celebrate; it was an opportunity. Every small step forward was a win and a chance.

While Grant was in the hospital, asking myself what I could do tomorrow helped me focus on what was within my power instead of the countless things that were out of my control. I had no power over how quickly Grant came out of the coma, but I was in charge of whether or not I was present at the hospital every day, interacting with doctors and advocating for my son. That was huge. Once his feeding tube was out, I could control what Grant ate, so I dragged that cooler full of nutritious food with me to the hospital every day and made sure the nurses knew not to feed Grant hospital food. I could control what Grant heard about his prognosis, how his senses were stimulated, and whether or not his ears and mind were filled with words of love and support. These things may have been minor compared to the major health issues Grant was facing, but they compounded over time, leading to a tidal wave of positive change.

Looking at the canyon, I wondered what small changes, which little hinges, I might have been missing now that no one was there to point them out to me. I realized that on this trip, instead of tuning in to all the tiny ways Grant was progressing as I had in the hospital by asking myself what went well today and what I could do tomorrow, I was being too rigid about my goals. I was so intent on Grant's being happy on vacation that I was failing to notice what was actually making him happy.

Now that I finally stopped and asked myself, I realized that a lot of things had gone well each day on our trip. Grant enjoyed our meals together. He and Bryce were getting along. He liked being in the condo. Wasn't that enough?

For the rest of the trip, I made an effort to let go of my preconceived notions about what Grant should be enjoying and let him be free to actually enjoy himself.

At the end of each day, I considered my key questions: "What went well today?" and "What else can I do?" Of course, not only was Grant happier when I stopped nagging him and let him do what he wanted, but I was happier too. I was finally able to truly enjoy my adventures with Bryce, our meals together as a family, and even our downtime in the condo. It was a relief to let go of the pressure I'd put on all of us to have fun and just have fun.

When he wasn't playing video games in the condo, Grant was drawing. He sketched dozens of images of the island's landscape and its tropical birds, and I could see his skill evolving from one piece of art to the next. I was so grateful that I'd tuned in to the small shifts Grant was making when I did so that I noticed and truly appreciated these small yet meaningful improvements.

Shortly after we got home from our vacation, I sat down with John, Grant, and Bryce to watch a documentary called *The Crash Reel*. The movie told the story of champion snowboarder Kevin Pearce, who was a strong contender to win the gold medal in the 2010 Olympics before sustaining an accident while training that left him with a devastating brain injury. Ever since Grant's accident, people had been telling me about Kevin. *The Crash Reel* told the story of Kevin's early snowboarding career, his accident, and his long road to recovery. I could see right away why my friends had been encouraging me to watch it. Though their accidents were vastly different, there were a lot of similarities between Kevin and Grant.

As I watched, one of the things that stood out to me the most was the way Kevin's family responded to the accident. Kevin's father,

Simon, watched the drip that was managing the pressure on Kevin's brain. The doctors had told him that the clearer the fluid, the better. "For weeks, I just watched that drip," he said, "to see if it was clear." I remembered how happy I had felt when the drip from Grant's brain slowly began to drain less and less fluid. This was one of the first signs that Grant's brain was starting to heal. At the time, it was a miracle. It was everything.

Like Grant, Kevin slowly came out of his coma one small step at a time. And like me, Kevin's parents continued to celebrate each tiny sign of progress along the way. "When I was sitting with him, holding his hand, he moved his finger in the palm of my hand," Simon said. "We were so happy."

After almost a month, Kevin moved from the intensive care unit to acute care. He was by no means out of the woods. Yet his mother smiled gratefully. "This is a good day," she said on the day of the transfer. It reminded me of the Facebook post I'd written describing what a good day it had been when Grant simply sighed.

By the time the movie ended, I had tears streaming down my face. Watching *The Crash Reel* was more painful than I had imagined it would be, but it was also inspiring. It reminded me how important it had been in the early days after Grant's accident to celebrate the small wins and focus on what I could control. Kevin's family and I had been forced to adopt that mindset by extreme circumstances. Noticing each small shift, from a finger squeeze to an eyelid flutter, gave us hope and kept us going during the darkest times in our sons' recoveries. But what if we brought this same approach to every part of our lives?

I kept this idea in mind as I continued holding question-and-answer sessions with readers. For the first time, I noticed how frequently they started the calls by telling me about everything they were doing wrong. Before they even asked me any questions, they often began by apologizing for themselves. "I had a bad week," they would say. "I went out for my coworker's birthday and couldn't resist the cake, so I just decided to throw in the towel and start over next week."

By focusing on what went wrong, they had destroyed their own hope before they even really got started. With the idea of celebrating the small wins in mind, I made sure to ask them about what had gone right. "What went well today?" I asked. "Did you drink any extra water this week or squeeze in an extra serving or two of vegetables?"

When faced with these questions, they almost always found something positive to share. "That's wonderful," I told them when they did. "Over time, those small changes will have an enormous impact on your health."

It often wasn't until I pointed out what had gone well that they became aware of their effects. "You know, I did have a little bit more energy this week," they said. Or "I could still fit into my jeans, even right after they got out of the dryer!" I ended those calls feeling confident that paying attention to those small shifts would motivate my readers to keep going in the right direction. This would undoubtedly lead to greater and greater change as time went on.

Just a few weeks later, in early August, I put on my second Mindshare Summit. The first one had been a success, but there was so much more that I wanted to accomplish with this group. It was clear to me that each of these talented people could broaden their reach and continue helping more and more people, and I was determined to help them do it.

At this event, we had 50 percent more participants, which to me was a big win. Among the new guests were Dave Asprey, the entrepreneur and biohacker behind the Bulletproof Diet, and Randy Hartnell, the founder and CEO of Vital Choice Seafood. With the idea of celebrating the small wins fresh in my mind, I could see how this lesson related directly to both Dave's and Randy's journeys.

Randy, who spent decades as a wild salmon fisherman, had the idea to start a company that would deliver wild salmon and other high-quality seafood to customers' doors after the advent of farmed salmon put him out of business. When he lost his livelihood, Randy sank into a depression, but he soon found that when he ate more of the wild salmon he had spent so many years fishing, his brain was so well nourished that he literally couldn't think a negative thought. I smiled when I heard this, thinking of course of the fish oil we'd given Grant in the hospital. It was amazing to think that something as simple as fish oil could really have played such a big role in his recovery.

Next, Dave shared the story of how he'd first gotten into biohacking. As a successful but overweight young entrepreneur, Dave found that his brain had stopped working the way he expected it to. He couldn't focus, had trouble retaining new information, and suffered from chronic, debilitating fatigue that couldn't be explained away by an entrepreneur's lack of sleep.

"It felt like something was broken in my brain," he said. "As if I had a constant hangover." His brain fog and exhaustion left him irritable and cranky, quick to anger and impulsive decisions. It felt like he had to work twice as hard as other people to get the same amount done. "My hardware was failing," he told me, "and I needed to take drastic measures to upgrade."

Dave spent the next decade on a journey to hack his brain and his body to uncover the secrets to greater resilience. This meant measuring his physical output and experimenting to troubleshoot the environment around him—and inside him—to see what factors were influencing his performance. It was fascinating to hear how this had forced Dave to take note of even the smallest changes that were taking place.

As he experimented with every conceivable method that might upgrade his performance—from oxygen masks and lasers to brain training software, neurofeedback, breathing exercises, electrical stimulation, ice baths, yoga, meditation, and every possible supplement—he continued measuring his body's output. This way, he could see clearly if a given technique was affecting his performance, even if the change was so subtle that he couldn't feel it. This was his way of asking himself what was going well and what else he could do to aim for even better.

"That's so interesting," I told Dave. "One of the things that really got me through when Grant was in the hospital was taking note of what went well each day."

Dave just stared at me. "Have I told you that I do that with my kids?" he asked me. "Every night before bed, we each go around and share three wins from the day. Their answers are hilarious," Dave continued, laughing. "They give me great insight into what's going on in my kids' minds, and it keeps me in a constant state of gratitude. Of all the crazy hacks I've tried, that one thing has had a bigger impact on my life than almost anything else."

I was dumbfounded to learn that while our situations were drastically different, Dave and I both relied on remarkably similar techniques to stay grateful and positive. This was clearly something that could help people face a wide variety of challenges. For some of us it may have been just waking up on this planet, but we could all find something that was going well each day that we could be grateful for.

This was the fourth lesson, an essential part of the Miracle Mindset—celebrating the small wins each day while moving forward toward big goals. This keeps you focused on living in gratitude every day.

Later that night, I hosted a big dinner for the attendees in the hotel's ballroom. From the corner of the room I watched this group of brilliant and powerful guests mingling and having fun, and I was flooded with gratitude. Just being among them was an honor, and as I looked around the room I was aware of how much each of these people had helped me in the past year—whether it was by sending food to the hospital, saying a prayer for Grant, or sharing the Virgin Diet with their followers. I owed a piece of my success—and Grant's—to each one of them.

"Hi, everyone," I said in a loud voice, interrupting their conversations. "I just want to thank you all for being here. This has been a transformative event, and I'm so grateful to you all for playing a role in that." I took a breath, feeling a bit nervous about what I was going to say next. "And on a personal note," I continued, "I want you all to know how much your support has meant to me over the past year. You've all been praying for Grant and asking me how he is, and I wanted you to see firsthand how much you've helped." I walked across the room to a big set of double doors and opened it wide. "So here he is!"

Grant, Bryce, and John walked into the room, each of them smiling widely as they took in the roomful of astonished guests. They all stood up at their tables and started applauding and cheering as some wiped tears from their eyes. I just stood off to the side and watched, my heart swelling. It had never felt so full. Bryce nudged Grant, encouraging him to say something. Grant raised his right arm and waved, the smile never leaving his face. "Hi, everyone," he said.

Once things calmed down a bit, a few guests took a moment to speak to Grant one-on-one. Leanne Ely approached him and shared a story that I'd heard many times before. Over twenty years earlier, Leanne threw a baby shower for her best friend. The baby was due in just a few weeks, and when the mother-to-be went to the bathroom just before the shower, she started bleeding. Leanne knew instinctively that something was very wrong. "We have to get to the hospital right now," she said, but her friend didn't want to ruin the shower that Leanne had spent so much time planning and insisted that she was fine.

Leanne didn't listen. She drove her friend to the hospital, where the doctors said that if they had waited another five minutes, both the baby and mother would have died. Both of them were saved, but when the baby was born, the doctors said he was severely brain-damaged.

"No, he's not," Leanne said simply. In her heart, she knew the baby would be fine. This gave the mother a small bit of hope, which she clung to as she tried to tune out the doctors' negative predictions. Knowing that it means warrior, she decided to name the baby Grant.

Over the next several years, baby Grant thrived. His brain was not damaged at all, and he grew into a brilliant young man who was his high school's valedictorian and received the prestigious Morehead Scholarship to the University of North Carolina, Chapel Hill.

In the hotel ballroom, Leanne took my Grant's hands in hers and looked him in the eye. "I believe you have the same grace that baby Grant had twenty years ago," she told him. "You're my Grant to pray for now."

Grant reached out and pulled Leanne into a tight hug. When they separated, I saw tears in his eyes. I was surprised by how much Leanne's story had affected Grant. This was a new side of him— sensitive, empathetic. That in and of itself was yet another win.

I returned home from that summit feeling more motivated than ever to revel in each small step Grant made on his way toward 110 percent. I still believed that he would get there. The one area where his progress could most clearly be seen was still his art. Every time Grant showed me a new drawing, I tried to find something new that he had done well. Sometimes it was as simple as using more texture or greater detail. Other times it was how lifelike the animals and insects that he drew looked, as if they were about to leap or fly off the page.

I noticed that the more I praised these incremental changes, the more they compounded. Grant went from drawing what he saw to seeking out new images to re-create. He often asked me what he should draw, and I tried to make my suggestions increasingly difficult so that he would continue challenging himself and keep getting better. Over time he went from drawing a simple sunflower to the intricate blooms of a rose. As he finished each new piece, I asked Grant what he thought had gone well and what else he could do tomorrow. This encouraged him to begin upping the ante for himself, researching each flower and learning its name and how to spell it before beginning to draw.

"Good job, honey," I told him when he handed me his latest piece, a lovely and lifelike sketch of a hydrangea with the name spelled correctly underneath. He still wasn't getting any closer to graduating from high school, and he wasn't the Grant I had once known. But as I looked at him, I knew that he was evolving invisibly in that moment, as we all were. Every breath that escaped from his lungs and every miraculous beat of his heart was a tiny, seemingly inconsequential hinge, but little hinges swing big doors.

WARRIOR MOM'S MANTRA

Big changes for the better are actually made up of so many little shifts in attitude and actions. Instead of focusing on what's going wrong, help your family celebrate their wins! That gratitude is key not only to happy parents, but to kids who grow up positive and resilient.

12

If You Want to Take the Island, Burn All the Boats

After the Mindshare Summit, I spent some time talking to Randy Hartnell, the founder of Vital Choice Seafood. I had known Randy for years, but I didn't know the story behind his business or how he became so passionate about wild seafood.

Randy told me that had spent over twenty years as a wild salmon fisherman in Alaska. He was good at what he did, and found it adventurous and fulfilling. Then, seemingly overnight, his entire industry changed. Randy suddenly faced intense competition from the farmed salmon industry, which pushed the price of wild salmon down so low that Randy could no longer sustain a living.

"I lost my livelihood, my community, and my identity along with my source of income," he told me. "I couldn't support my family, and as the bills piled up and debt collectors started calling, I became very depressed." Randy paused for a moment. "It got so bad that at one point I seriously considered ending it all."

For Randy, finding a way to use his expertise to earn a living was a matter of life or death, and he treated it as such.

Not only was Randy in a dire situation, but he also believed strongly in the product he'd learned so much about over the years. He knew that wild salmon was superior to farmed salmon both nutritionally and environmentally, and he was certain that if consumers were educated about the differences and had access to wild salmon, they would choose it.

"Because the situation was so desperate, I felt that the radar in my brain that sensed opportunities was turned way up," he told me. Randy searched for solutions and used every tool at his disposal to solve the problem.

While his fellow fishermen got jobs in oil refineries and encouraged Randy to join them, he chose a different route. He decided to start a business called Vital Choice Seafood that would ship wild salmon directly to people's homes. It was a huge risk, but Randy went all in and committed to his business succeeding. His life was at stake, and there was no other option.

It was challenging and certainly scary, but when Randy started getting letters from customers saying how grateful they were for his product, he gained the courage to keep pushing. His business grew year after year and became more gratifying and financially rewarding than he'd ever imagined.

"When I first heard what happened to Grant," Randy told me after finishing his story, "I knew right away that it would fuel you to make your book even bigger than it would have been otherwise."

I couldn't stop thinking about what Randy had said. Intuitively, I sensed that he was right. I had no doubt that Grant's accident played a role in making *The Virgin Diet* as successful as it was. But how? What exactly would I have done differently if everything had gone according to plan? Of course I wanted my next book to be just as successful (this time hopefully without one of my sons' lives on the line), so I was determined to figure it out.

I thought about Randy's story again. The key to the success of Randy's business seemed to be the intense level of his commitment. I'd seen so many other entrepreneurs start a business with the mindset of "I'll see what happens." This gave them an out, an excuse to fail, and they usually already had a Plan B in place in case they did. But Randy had no backup plan, and therefore no choice but to succeed. He started his business with the intention that "I must succeed no matter what." He couldn't give up because he didn't feel like doing the work it would take to succeed. He had to do whatever it took.

Likewise, with *The Virgin Diet* I didn't just *want* the book to succeed; I *needed* it to succeed. Even before Grant's accident, I was fully invested. I had spent my entire book advance and taken on additional debt to create the public television special and to promote the book. I wasn't approaching the book launch thinking *I hope this works*. Instead, my back was against the wall. If it failed, no one was going to bail me out. I would be penniless and unable to support my kids and myself. It *had* to work.

Grant's accident raised the stakes even higher. Now there were medical bills that listed numbers I couldn't comprehend, plus the cost of Grant's therapy when he got out of the hospital and the uncertainty about his needs for the future. In the early days after his accident, I didn't know if he would remain in a coma indefinitely, be immobile and in need of constant medical care for the rest of his life, or if he would ever be financially independent. All I knew was that I wasn't going to let finances stop me from getting him whatever he needed to recover. There's never been a better motivator than that.

But it wasn't enough to go all in for the book. I had to go all in for Grant himself. When I looked at him lying unconscious in that hospital bed, I knew that I had a choice. I could choose to shoot for good enough, or I could take a risk and commit to aiming for great. That's when I decided that Grant was going to come out of this better than ever.

I believed I would get what I expected and that he would too, so I made sure to fill Grant's ears with words of hope and possibility. My intention was that when—not if—he woke up, he'd take a risk and commit to greatness with hope and possibility in mind. We'd share the same commitment to greatness, and that idea fueled me through every stage of his recovery.

I woke up every day and asked myself what I could do to help get Grant to 110 percent. This led to a completely different course of action than if my commitment had merely been for him to survive. If I had given myself an out, would I have insisted that the doctors treat his heel as if it were Kobe Bryant's? Would I have worked so hard to protect Grant from the devastating trauma that was going on around him? Perhaps most important, would I have made my own health a priority and made sure that I got enough nutrition, sleep, and exercise to focus and be fully present at every moment to make the decisions that would ultimately determine the course of his life?

To me, a good outcome for Grant was nonnegotiable, and so was the success of *The Virgin Diet*. In order for me to provide for Grant both in the short term and the long term, the book had to be a success. And so, just as I woke up each morning asking myself what I could do for Grant, I did everything I could each day to make the book launch huge. I knew that the information in the book could change the world, and I was looking at being bankrupt if it didn't work. I believed in what I was doing so much that I went all in. I didn't have a backup plan because I wasn't planning to fail.

Of course, in the back of my mind every day was this truth: maybe it wouldn't work. The statistics showed that Grant probably wouldn't make it, and I knew the chances of the book succeeding were pretty slim too. Most likely, it would land on the bookshelves along with thousands of others, and no one would notice or care. There was just as good a chance that Grant would never make it to 110 percent. He might have gotten only half that far, or maybe he wouldn't get anywhere at all.

But I also knew there was a chance this really could be the best thing that ever happened to Grant. It was also possible, however unlikely, that the book would succeed beyond my wildest dreams and change millions of lives. So I held on to those chances with everything I had. As long as there was a chance, I had hope.

Facing a life-and-death situation with my son had frightened me to my core, but I was beginning to realize how powerful that fear had been. I was scared every single day in the hospital—scared that Grant would die, scared that Grant would survive only to live a difficult and painful life, scared that the book would fail, and scared that we'd end up broke. With that fear putting my back against the wall, I had to succeed. That fear was my fuel. Whether I wanted to or not, I had no choice but to take the steps that would give Grant and the book their best chance. Once I made the decision to go all in for both of them, I couldn't back out no matter how scary things got.

Luckily, I had already gotten comfortable facing my fears.

Years before, after doing the work to rid myself of my limiting beliefs and getting to the next level in my career, I wanted to learn how to take bigger risks. As an entrepreneur, I've always been a bit of a risk taker, but I wasn't yet comfortable taking big risks in my career.

I could barely afford to pay my mortgage while going through the divorce when I joined my business coach Ali Brown's mastermind group. I didn't have the money to join, but I knew that if I wanted to do better in my career, I couldn't keep doing the things that weren't working. I had to believe in myself enough to go all in.

Working with Ali, I went from speaking to small groups and working one-on-one with weight-loss clients to leading large online events and stepping out in a much more public way. I was scared each time I stretched myself, but the risks started paying off in the form of great results and positive feedback. There were also some haters along the way who made me doubt myself, but I had no safety net and no choice but to keep pushing forward.

Over time I became more comfortable taking bigger and bigger risks that each forced me to step up to a new level. When facing a risk, I stopped looking at the failure statistics and started considering only the potential of any project I took on. I used to panic at the idea of having $10,000 in business debt, but as the risks I was taking began to pay off, I got better at evaluating them and more comfortable taking bigger ones. All of a sudden, I didn't even flinch taking the type of risk that had once seemed like such a big deal.

By the time Grant's accident happened, I had nearly a million dollars invested in *The Virgin Diet*, which was by far the biggest business risk I'd ever taken. By then I had reframed my fear. It was now my litmus test. Whenever I was afraid, I knew I was stretching myself. If I felt comfortable, I was playing it safe. This meant it was time to make a commitment to a bigger and scarier goal.

I hadn't realized while Grant was in the hospital that I was drawing on those same risk-taking muscles as I fought for his life. When I went against the advice of the doctor and insisted on having Grant airlifted to undergo the risky surgery to repair his aorta, I was scared. I was taking Grant's recovery into my own hands. But when that risk paid off and he survived, I gained the confidence to take more risks by pushing the hospital to give him fish oil, start him on rehabilitation therapy, and ultimately discharge him sooner than his doctors originally advised.

It all started with that commitment—my scary stretch goal to get Grant to 110 percent—and then everything flowed naturally from there. When I really dialed in on that commitment, all sorts of help started showing up. Out of nowhere, people began contacting me about things like essential oils, progesterone, and fish oil. Perhaps this was because, as had happened with Randy, my commitment had turned my radar that sensed opportunities all the way up. I was open to anything that wasn't potentially harmful, and this openness empowered me to take the necessary steps to follow through and reach my goal.

Going all in also forced me to become laser focused and eliminate anything from my life that wasn't related to my two priorities: Grant and the book. Because of those two things, another top priority was my own self-care. A lot of people didn't understand this. Why would I take the time to go to the gym and source healthy food when my son was in a coma? But I needed to be all the way on at every moment to make potentially life-altering decisions while Grant was in the hospital, and if I had felt tired, unfocused, or uncomfortable in my own skin, it would have been impossible for me to be fully present. Having enough energy to function at my best was literally a matter of life and death.

Some of my friends who visited me in the hospital saw how I was functioning and said, "You're Superwoman," but my response was "No, I'm super healthy." If I hadn't been on the top of my game before Grant's accident and continued to take care of myself, my son wouldn't have still been alive. I wouldn't have had the confidence, energy, or presence of mind to do what I had to do to succeed, and the result would have been a very different outcome.

When Grant's accident forced me to become laser focused on

the things that really mattered, I realized that my endless to-do list could have been trimmed down to a few essential items all along. I only wish I could have done this sooner. I already knew before the accident that I was failing my boys and myself by not being present, but I didn't have a compelling-enough reason to make a change. I knew I could do better, but I was comfortable with the status quo, and it unfortunately took Grant's accident to serve as a big wake-up call to make a change.

I realized that when we're comfortable, we often don't take things as seriously as we should. We become complacent. Whether it's by fully investing financially or emotionally in a big, scary goal, it takes getting a little uncomfortable to force ourselves to do the necessary work to succeed. There is no way to start a business, save a life, or just push further without taking an enormous leap of faith. Progress requires risk; it's as simple as that. That risk has to mean something; it has to be worth it, and when you make that progress nonnegotiable, you have no choice but to face the fear and take that risk.

A few weeks later, I was on the phone with a friend, who told me, "There's an amazing event coming up in New York that you should go to." She said that the marketing guru Joe Polish was hosting a Genius Network event with some of the world's biggest entrepreneurs. I was intrigued. Ever since I had begun speaking, I was always looking for new opportunities, and this sounded promising. I also knew that in order for me to get to the next level in my business,

I needed to spend time with people who thought bigger than me. Then she said that the event cost $10,000, and everyone paid to attend, whether they were speaking or not.

"No way," I said immediately. "I wouldn't pay that much money to attend a two-day seminar, let alone pay to speak at it!"

She persisted. "There will be amazing people there," she told me. "It's really hard to get to speak there, and I got you in. I promise it will be worth it."

I had an intuitive hit that I was supposed to be there. It was a risk, but maybe this was a good opportunity to make myself un-comfortable and eliminate the status quo. Maybe it wouldn't pay off, but there was a small chance that going to this event would. That chance was all I needed.

On the day of the event, I felt that familiar fear creeping up on me. At most of my events and speaking engagements, I was used to being the big fish in a small pond, but in this room of international CEOs and leaders, I was a minnow. I was nothing. But that fear told me that I was doing something right, so I gathered my courage and walked in.

In the back of my mind, I was entertaining the idea of scrapping my typical speech about nutrition and talking about everything I had been through with Grant. I knew this was another risk, but I thought it would be a good chance for me to see if our story would resonate with others. As I sat there listening to business speech after business speech, I changed my mind. There was no way I could speak about something so personal in front of this intimidating group. I slowly grew more and more nervous. These were huge power players, household names. What right did I have to be there? To make matters worse, I was the very last speaker of the event.

As we broke for lunch, a woman who had been sitting right in front of me throughout the event turned around and introduced herself. She was nearly as tall as me and beautiful, with a wide smile. "I'm Renee Airya," she said. "What are you going to speak about?"

I told her that I was torn between my usual nutrition speech and the much more personal talk about Grant. "What about you?" I asked.

Renee looked at me with knowing brown eyes. "It's about something I call flipping your flaws," she said. "I'd be very curious to hear what you think."

Renee spoke right after the lunch break. She had hinted that her speech would be personal, but I had no idea how powerful it would be. Just a few years before, Renee was at the height of her career as an international model when she was diagnosed with a rare and life-threatening brain tumor. After undergoing emergency surgery to remove the tumor, she was told that the tumor had been the only thing holding her facial nerve together. Removing it had left her completely paralyzed on the right side of her face. Just like that, Renee lost her career, her identity, and her ability to smile.

Renee refused to believe that she would never regain movement in her face. Even though the doctors told her that it was medically impossible, she completely committed herself to learning to smile again within six months. She had no safety net or backup plan—her smile was her most prized physical and soulful feature—and she approached her goal as if it were a matter of life and death.

Every day for six months, Renee spent hours doing facial exercises, visualizations, and meditating. Day after day, there was no improvement, but she didn't give up. And then just days before the six months were up, a miracle happened. "One day I felt the tiniest spark," she said. "If I hadn't been spending so much time doing exercises in front of the mirror, I probably wouldn't even have felt it." Renee kept pushing forward and ultimately recovered 60 percent of the movement in her face. Better yet, she now used her story to inspire others and encourage them to see their biggest flaws as their greatest assets.

I sat there with tears in my eyes. Like Randy—and like me when Grant was in the hospital—Renee had committed herself fully to the outcome she wanted, even if that commitment came with an enormous amount of risk and uncertainty. This, I realized as I wiped away my tears, was an essential part of the Miracle Mindset and one of the greatest secrets to success: Instead of getting a little bit pregnant with an idea or trying your hand at something, you make a big commitment and then you never give up. Block off the exit doors and destroy your safety net. If you want to take the island, burn all the boats.

Finally it was my turn to speak. "I'm so excited to introduce you guys to JJ Virgin," Joe Polish said from the stage. "She is going to talk to you all about nutrition and getting healthy."

I took a breath, walked onto the stage, and looked out at the intimidating group of mostly men in the audience. *They don't need to hear about nutrition,* I thought. If Renee could get her face to move again, I could certainly take a risk and talk about my son.

Over the next ten minutes, I told the audience about everything I'd gone through with Grant and the lessons I had begun to piece together in the aftermath of the accident—the importance of celebrating the small wins; taking action, however small or imperfect it may be; breaking free of self-imposed limits; and going all in. I had no notes and nothing prepared. I spoke straight from the heart. When my ten minutes were up, I stopped to catch my breath and looked at the crowd of power players in the audience. They were clearly moved. In fact, some of the strong, powerful men were openly crying.

As I returned to my seat, I realized that if the Miracle Mindset had helped me save Grant and launch a bestseller, there were probably a lot of people outside of this room who could benefit from hearing our story too. What had happened to Grant was unique, but the lessons I'd learned from the experience were universal. Perhaps our story could inspire other people to recover from an illness, finally lose the weight they'd been carrying for too long, overcome a major obstacle, or just push forward to the next level of their careers.

Just a few days later, Grant and I were playing Ping-Pong after a long day at work when Grant put his paddle down and rested both of his hands on the table. "You know, Mom," he said casually, "when I was in the coma, the gray man came and asked if I wanted to live or die."

I stood still and listened to him. Grant had made a few references to the things he had seen and heard while he was in the coma, but this was the first time he'd mentioned this.

"I didn't really want to live," he continued, "but I just kept hearing you."

Grant picked up his paddle and hit the ball across the table to me. It went right off the side, scoring Grant a point, and he smiled. I just stood there, frozen. Was it possible that he had really heard me talking to him the whole time he was in the coma, just as I had hoped? A big part of me had doubted all along whether it was making a difference, but maybe my commitment to filling his ears with words of love and support really had played a role in saving Grant's life by pulling him out of the "gray man's" grasp and back into the world of the living.

If this were the case, then my refusal to let anyone speak a negative word about Grant's prognosis in his presence must have made a difference too. He had awoken with the expectation of recovering to 110 percent, because that was the only possible outcome he'd ever heard.

My phone rang, interrupting our Ping-Pong game. My assistant was in a panic because we had miscalculated the shipping costs of some products. It was a $50,000 mistake, which was huge. This was the kind of thing I would have gotten all worked up about when the boys were little. After all, I didn't have an extra $50,000 lying around to fix this problem. But on that day, I just shrugged. Grant was alive, the book had succeeded, and all was well. Everything else seemed inconsequential. I could find a way to fix this.

"Don't worry," I told my assistant. "It's not a matter of life and death."

It had always been so easy for me to get hung up on things and worry incessantly, and this was a powerful new benchmark. Asking myself if something that seemed like a huge problem was a matter of life and death made my priorities crystal clear. Was this something I would be willing to go all in for? If not, then it didn't matter. It was just a distraction. Was it fixable? If so, then it was nothing to worry about.

Of course, I might have never learned this lesson if the past year had been different. It had taken having my son's life on the line for me to see what really mattered.

Looking at Grant, I realized that he had learned this too. This was why he was so hung up on finding his purpose. He had chosen to live and fought his way back from the brink of death for a reason. It was a matter of life and death to figure out what it was. I served the ball back to Grant, determined to continue treating everything in my life with the exact amount of importance that it warranted. This meant not worrying about things that were fixable and taking risks and going all in when it really mattered. I wouldn't have wished what we had been through during the last year on anyone, but I was tremendously grateful that both Grant and I had learned this lesson.

Warrior Mom's Mantra

Courage isn't about being fearless—it's about being open to possibilities, even when life is scary and unpredictable. Moms have the unique chance to help our families see challenges as opportunities. We can lean in and use our fear as inspiration to reach even higher.

13

A Rising Tide Lifts All Boats

As we approached the holiday season, I found myself falling into a bit of a funk. Over a year had passed since Grant's accident. It had been the best and the worst year of my life. Grant had survived. In many ways, he really was better than ever. He was more creative, gentle, empathetic, and kind. I was better too. I felt more confident than ever and had grown closer to my family and friends. *The Virgin Diet* had also succeeded to a greater extent than I'd ever imagined.

And yet in many ways I was still recovering from the post-traumatic stress of almost losing my son. I was often more emotional and in general more vulnerable. I felt like I'd been cracked open, and an essential piece of me that had been hidden until now had finally emerged. I knew this was a good thing, but that didn't make it any less painful. Speaking to other people both publicly and privately about everything I had learned in the aftermath of Grant's accident was helpful. But there were still plenty of days when I longed to shut the door, put this all behind me, and never think about anything related to the accident ever again.

Bryce was now in his junior year of high school and was beginning to think ahead to college. Grant was seventeen. He should have been in his senior year. His friends were consumed with college tours and applications, and his future was still a complete unknown. I had struggled to let go of my hope for him to finish high school, but now it was hard to move forward without a clear goal or vision for the future. The question "Now what?" hung over our house and remained unanswered.

Grant felt this too. As his outbursts had continued to subside, he had slowly gained more independence. His main complaint now was a lack of purpose, yet he did nothing to help himself find one. He stopped doing the assignments from his tutor, sat at home, and played video games. His speech therapist, Marcey, was still his one and only friend.

I constantly wondered if Grant's lack of drive was a side effect of the traumatic brain injury, a symptom of his bipolar disorder, or just Grant being Grant. He was still a teenager, after all. I knew it wasn't uncommon for a boy his age to feel purposeless, but without a clear-cut future for him to look forward to, it was more problematic than usual.

On Thanksgiving Grant took his plate of food into his room and refused to come with us to visit some friends for dessert. "Come on, honey, it will be good for you to get out," I told him as I leaned against the outside of his bedroom door.

"You don't get it, Mom," he whined, sounding very much like his preaccident self. "I have no purpose. Why am I even here?"

This was awful to hear. Grant clearly knew he had told the "gray man" that he wanted to live for a reason, but he didn't yet know what it was. I thought about the holiday season the year before, when Grant was at Children's Hospital. I remembered walking through halls decorated for Christmas and seeing kids who were years younger than Grant walking slowly down the hallway, wheeling their chemotherapy IV carts.

I often went straight from the hospital to a studio to shoot a television appearance. On the way, I listened to cars honking and drivers swearing at each other. If I stopped at the store to grab something, I saw people fighting over on-sale sweaters or stuffed animals. I wished that all of these people would take one hour during the holiday season to hand out gifts at Children's Hospital and see what went on in there. They'd stop all that pettiness immediately and realize what really mattered.

If Grant needed a purpose, then maybe this was the answer for him too. A few days later I took him to the toy store and told him to pick out dozens of toys. They weren't for him, but that didn't make it any less fun. Grant ran around the toy store gleefully throwing Lego sets, race cars, books, video games, and puzzles into a cart. Then we went home and wrapped everything. The next day we went back to a place I thought I'd never set foot in again—Children's Hospital Los Angeles.

John and I stood a few feet behind Grant as he walked confidently through the double doors leading into the hospital. The first time he'd passed through those doors, he was in a wheelchair, could barely feed himself, and didn't know his own name. The change in him was incredible.

We made our way to the acute rehabilitation unit where Grant had once been treated and sat down in a main area where it would be easy for people to congregate while Grant handed out gifts to the kids. Several doctors, nurses, and other therapists trickled in to get a look at Grant. The expressions on their faces told me how thrilled they were to see a patient come full circle. I knew that very few patients in Grant's condition ever recovered to this extent.

"What a treat," Dr. Craig said as he crossed the room to shake Grant's hand. "What brings you back to see us, Grant?"

Grant smiled at Dr. Craig in recognition. The blank stare and confusion were gone. "I wanted to do something to help," Grant said, "and to just show the kids that it takes time, but they will get better."

Dr. Craig couldn't hide how surprised he was to hear the improvement in Grant's speech. "Amazing," he said to John and me as patients gathered around and Grant proudly began handing out presents. Seeing the joy on each of their faces made Grant smile from ear to ear. "This is why we do what we do," Dr. Craig told me, "and to see this kind of success story is unbelievable."

A quiet girl just about Grant's age approached him in a wheelchair. "Hi, I'm Erica," she said. I watched Grant as he took in the girl's shaved head, which was covered by a brightly colored scarf, and the IV sticking out of her arm.

"Hi, Erica, I'm Grant," he said, handing her a present.

Across the room, I noticed a man and a woman I assumed were her parents with tears in their eyes as they watched Erica and Grant continue talking. I could tell just by looking at them that their daughter's prognosis was bad. I recognized the expressions on their faces all too well. Walking across the room to them, I introduced myself. "Merry Christmas," I told them.

"That is the work of the Lord," the woman said in response, gesturing toward Grant. "That is a miracle."

The couple, Mike and Dana, introduced themselves and told me that they had traveled to Los Angeles from their home in Guam to get Erica the best possible treatment for her rare form of cancer.

"Thank God Erica is in remission," Dana told me, "but the doctors say she still has an underlying disease. It's just really hard." Her voice broke and she shook her head, wiping away her tears.

"Forget what the doctors say," I told her, taking her hand. "They gave Grant no chance. But there's always a chance."

Dana nodded and struggled to smile. Then she told me that they had lost their son to the same disease just a few months before. He was only eleven years old. When he was diagnosed, Erica tested as a perfect match to be a bone marrow donor for her brother. It was during the routine pre-transplant testing that Erica was diagnosed with the very same disease her brother was suffering from. She went from trying to save her brother to fighting for her own life. Her brother died just three months after his diagnosis.

Hearing what this family had already been through was shocking. It made Grant's accident seem like a walk in the park. As we continued talking, Mike mentioned that they had three other daughters who were still back at home in Guam, staying with their extended family. They couldn't afford to fly them all here to be with Erica. Mike and Dana had both been out of work for several months since their son was first diagnosed. They had been forced to leave their jobs to be at his side, and were now staying at the nearby Ronald McDonald House while Erica was being treated at Children's Hospital.

"The girls were all so close," Mike told me. "I just hope that Erica has a chance to see her sisters again. It's the first Christmas since we lost our son, and the thought of not spending it together . . ." He trailed off as he took his wife's hand in his own.

Looking back toward Erica and Grant, I saw the image of Grant and Bryce when Grant was just starting to come out of the coma and Bryce was trying to get Grant to raise his arm. "Raise your arm higher," Bryce told him over and over. Grant managed to get his arm up only about an inch or so higher each time. But Bryce knew how to motivate his brother better than anyone, and just before Grant gave up, Bryce stooped over just a few inches and snuck his shoulder underneath Grant's arm.

Back then, Grant's expression was often vacant, but I could see in his eyes how proud he was to have gotten his arm all the way up to his brother's shoulder. Would I have known to do that for Grant? Would John? I looked back at Mike and Dana without a moment's thought. "I'll fly them in," I told them.

Of course they resisted. "No," they said. "We can't ask you to do that."

"You're not asking," I told them. "I'm offering. And besides, I can probably use my frequent flyer miles." I immediately got on the phone with the airlines and found out that my miles didn't qualify. This was a difficult decision. The flights from Guam were very expensive, and I didn't have that extra money lying around. It would be a sacrifice, but I wasn't going to let money stop this girl from seeing her sisters—not if there was any way I could make it happen. I booked the flights and told her parents, "It's all taken care of."

"Seeing Grant brightened our day," Dana told me as we hugged. "But this . . . you'll never know how much this means to us."

"I do know," I told her. "That's why I'm doing it."

I said good-bye and went back to Grant so we could collect our things and head home. "How did that feel?" I asked him. I thought it must have been strange to see how everyone had reacted to his presence, touching him and looking at him in reverence as if he were walking hope.

"It felt good," Grant said with a smile. "It's something I feel really happy about."

It struck me that giving back had been one of the first things since the accident to make Grant truly happy. "Let's make it a tradition," I told him. Anything that made him smile like that was something we were going to do regularly.

Just a few days later Dana sent me a picture of Erica and her sisters during their reunion. I was dumbstruck to see the joy on the sisters' faces despite the circumstances and the light in Erica's eyes that had been missing just a few days before. Looking at that picture filled me with pure joy, and I found myself pulling it up on my phone again and again throughout my workday so I could look at it whenever I needed a little boost.

"How can we ever thank you?" Dana's message said. After staring at the image of her daughters for the tenth time that day, I responded honestly, "I should be the one thanking you."

When I'd offered to fly out Erica's sisters, I wasn't thinking about whether it would make me happy. I did it because it seemed like the least I could do for this family who had been through so much. But as I sent that message to Dana I realized how much giving to them had ended up doing for me. Helping that family in a relatively small way had given me so much hope and filled me with such joy. It made me want to be a better person. Is that what it had felt like for Grant to go back to the hospital and hand out presents?

I thought back to all the people who had helped me throughout the aftermath of Grant's accident—the strangers, friends, and family members alike. There was the family who had driven hours to pray over Grant; the people who simply said a prayer or sent a message of support; Dr. Meyer, who showed up with her essential oils; the countless people who emailed me with ideas about alternative treatments I could try; the friends who sent basket after basket of kale; and the people who showed up and sat next to me as I cried, held my hand, and just told me they loved me.

And then, of course, there was John. He had helped me more than anyone else throughout this entire journey. While we weren't a good fit as a married couple, we had worked together seamlessly in the hospital. We shared the same attitude about Grant's prognosis and balanced each other's temperaments better than we ever had before. When I got too aggressive with the doctors, John knew how to smooth it over. When I felt nauseated at the sight of bones and blood, John stepped in and acted as nurse, orderly, security guard, and dad. And when I needed to leave town for the book tour, John took over and stayed at Grant's bedside around the clock, often for days at a time. We had never been there for each other so much before, perhaps because we hadn't ever needed each other so badly.

Asking for and then willingly receiving all this help from each corner of my world went against my every instinct. For my entire life, I had prided myself on being strong and independent. Years before, when Susan had bailed me out of near bankruptcy, I couldn't bear the thought of accepting her help. What would that say about me, I wondered—that I was a helpless victim who couldn't run her own business? But I had no choice. I took the loan, and while I was incredibly grateful to Susan, I also felt guilty, indebted. I vowed to never need someone's help ever again.

In the years that passed before the night of Grant's accident, my business had grown, and I'd become even more independent than ever as an entrepreneur and the primary source of financial support for my sons. I was stubborn in my refusal of help from anyone. When I hosted dinner parties, I didn't let my guests bring so much as a bottle of wine. And at work, I took on way too much and then felt resentful of my team for not doing more to help me. But the truth is, I didn't let them step up and contribute as much as they could have because I wanted to feel like I could do it all by myself.

It's no coincidence that my business was based entirely around helping other people—both teaching them to live healthier lives and coaching health experts and entrepreneurs on how to grow their businesses. It felt great to see my clients lose weight, get healthier, or reach a wider audience and make a bigger impact. But now I realized that by always giving and never receiving, I was depriving the people in my life of the wonderful experience of stepping up and being there for someone else.

Grant's accident was so extreme that I had no choice but to ask for and accept help from anyone who was willing to give it to me. Posting a public message about Grant's accident took every bit of courage I had. I was terrified that I would be judged, that Grant would be judged, and that I would ultimately be let down. I wondered if my followers would think I was acting weak or opportunistic by asking for their help, or if they would criticize me for sharing such personal family information publicly. (And of course some people did, but only a small minority.)

I had no choice but to put those fears aside and reach out. Instead of micromanaging as I normally did and telling people what to do, I just asked for help. I didn't have any expectations about what would follow. I just knew that I needed support. Nearly everyone in my life showed up with whatever they felt they could contribute. They stepped up and surrounded me with love and support, and I was floored.

Along the way, I realized something about myself that I had never known before. For so many years I had prided myself on being strong and powerful. People often told me that I was intimidating, and I secretly liked hearing that. It made me feel in control. When I was finally forced to ask for help by the enormity of the situation I was facing with Grant, I realized that for all those years I had been hungry to be seen for who I really was.

The truth is, I'm not perfect. I can't always keep it together. Here was proof of that. And when I made that public and the people in my life showed up and supported me anyway, I realized that they cared about me despite my weaknesses. I felt truly, deeply adored for who I really was rather than for what I had accomplished. That was an amazing feeling, one that I realized I had been depriving myself of for too long.

Now I saw that if flying out Erica's sisters had brought me so much joy, maybe the people who'd been helping me throughout Grant's recovery were grateful for that opportunity too. When I started relying on my team more during Grant's recovery, they were able to rise to the next level and make a greater contribution to the company. That must have felt good.

I realized that throughout the past year I had been helping others by allowing them to help me. Asking for help was a form of charity. If this was the case, then it was completely off-balance for me to always be the one helping others. For too long I'd been acting selfishly by always giving to others and never offering them a chance to give back to me.

This realization reminded me of the conversation I had had with

Joe Polish at his Genius Network event in New York just a few
weeks before. Joe is a recovering addict. After a very difficult childhood during which his mother died and he was abused by a trusted
relative, Joe turned to drugs when he was a young teen.

"In eleventh grade I started smoking pot and doing speed, coke,
and acid, and eventually snorting crystal meth and freebasing," he
told me. "I became a really bad coke addict. I started feeling mentally better because the drugs took away a lot of my fear and social
anxiety. I went from being a shy, scared kid to being outgoing and
popular."

Over the years, Joe's addiction grew until he weighed just over a
hundred pounds and spent his entire day freebasing cocaine. When
another crazed addict burst into his room, poured lighter fluid all
over Joe, and threatened to light him on fire, Joe realized he had
two choices: he could leave or he would die. Joe got himself out of
that environment and spent the next two years getting clean. He
got a job selling health club memberships, and at that gym he met
a customer who ran a mental hospital. That customer offered Joe a
job as a mental health technician.

In addition to checking vital signs and working with patients,
Joe had to drive recovering addicts to Alcoholics Anonymous and
Narcotics Anonymous meetings. Joe sat in on those meetings and
absorbed the lessons that were being taught. The one that resonated
the most with Joe was the idea of being of service to others.

"One of the reasons that twelve-step programs work so well is
the service element," Joe told me. "If you feel hopeless, the best way
to get out of that is to be of service to other people." Just seeing how

his small contributions were helping the patients he drove to those meetings gave Joe a great deal of hope.

Over the next several years, Joe went from mental health technician to carpet cleaner to one of the most successful and renowned marketing gurus in the world.

Along the way, Joe never forgot to be of service to others. Whenever he found himself in a rut or being tempted by drugs, he found a way to be of service, whether it was by making a donation, talking to a veteran, or visiting a homeless shelter. These small acts of service always filled Joe with hope and kept him solidly on the path of recovery.

Joe learned—and now teaches—the incredible power of giving. "I got the best and healthiest high of my life from being of service to others," he told me. "But giving someone else a chance to experience that high is an even greater good."

Joe's last statement had stuck with me and confirmed what I was beginning to realize about accepting help—it was its own form of giving. By accepting his gifts, the children at Children's Hospital had helped Grant feel significant. By allowing me to fly in her daughters, Dana had given me hope and joy. And by asking the people around me for help, I had given them a chance to shine. This was the sixth piece of the Miracle Mindset—striking the right balance between giving help to and accepting help from others.

I began to view my ability to ask for help as a muscle. The more I exercised it, the stronger it would get. I started small. When I invited friends over, I told them exactly what to bring, and I found myself getting far less overwhelmed by the prospect of hosting. At work, I delegated everything that I didn't have to do myself, and my team continued to step up and shine. At home, I started asking Bryce and Grant for help, whether it was by straightening up, setting the table, or running basic errands. While there were still plenty of things Grant couldn't do himself, I found that as long as we came from a place of possibility, we could always find a way for him to help.

The more I did this, the prouder and more fulfilled Grant seemed when he was able to help me by performing simple tasks. By allowing Grant to help me, I was also helping him find his purpose, his reason for living—to help others.

When I saw this, I began encouraging Grant to come out with me more often so he could see the way people reacted to him. Sure enough, everywhere we went, people wanted to hug him and touch him and tell him their stories. His mere presence gave them hope. He was serving a powerful purpose simply by existing. And though Grant didn't always understand why people were so excited to talk to him and give him a hug, he naturally knew just what to say to perfect strangers to boost their spirits even more.

"She will get better," he told a woman whose granddaughter had been born with a rare genetic disorder. "Tell him to keep fighting," he told a man whose son was suffering from depression. "You will get through it, and he will too."

A few days later, I asked Grant to come with me to walk our dog, Daisy, to our neighbors' house. I was heading out of town the next day for a speaking engagement, and while I normally boarded Daisy at the kennel when I was out of town, this time I had a better idea.

My neighbors' kids adored Daisy and loved spoiling her with belly rubs any time they saw her out taking a walk. I knew their parents didn't want the responsibility of having their own dog, but maybe they could do me a favor by watching Daisy for a couple of days while enjoying the benefits of a part-time dog. This was a simple way of helping them by asking them to help me.

"Daisy!" the kids cried as soon as they saw her, dropping to their knees to indulge her with belly rubs. I watched them for a moment, smiling.

"I have a favor to ask you," I said to their mom. The more I practiced it, the easier it was for me to say this sentence. "Would you mind watching Daisy for me for the next two days? I have to go out of town, and I could really use the help."

She smiled and looked at her children, who were staring up at her with pleading eyes. "Of course," she said to me. "We would love that. Thank you!"

As we walked home in silence, Grant seemed lost in thought. "What's going on, honey?" I asked him. Grant looked up at me.

"When I told the gray man that I wanted to live," he said, "at first I thought I was going to live just for you. I wanted to live for you and Dad and Bryce." Grant was silent again for a moment. "But now I want to do more," he continued. "I want to help other people, but I don't know how. How can I help them when there are so many things I still can't even do?"

Before I responded, I thought about Erica and her family. I thought about the people Grant spoke to at the grocery store, and I thought about Joe, who was able to stay sober thanks in part to his ability to balance directly aiding others and indirectly helping them by giving them an opportunity to support him.

"You help people all the time without even realizing it," I told Grant. "You help them by giving them hope. You help them just by being you. And you help them by asking for help, by giving them a chance to help you." I put my arm around Grant as we continued walking. "Always remember to ask for help when you need it," I told him. "A rising tide lifts all boats."

WARRIOR MOM'S MANTRA

It's a blessing to give as a mom—to be there for your family, to help them navigate their world feeling loved and supported. But you know what? It's also a blessing to receive! Don't let being an amazing mom get in the way of accepting help. We're all in this together.

14

Forgiveness Will Set You Free

Since the fall, I had felt unsettled and generally down. Everything was going well, but the question "Now what?" just wouldn't go away. Though he enjoyed helping other people and giving them hope, Grant was still aimless, and for once I was at a loss for how to motivate him. I felt sapped of energy and inspiration, and I often wondered if I was suffering from some sort of post-traumatic stress disorder.

In mid-January, I hosted another Mindshare Summit. After seeing Grant at the last event, those who had attended wanted to know how he was doing. I wished I had something new to report, but the truth was, he was very much the same as when they'd seen him in August. When I answered honestly, the question that often followed took me by surprise: "Did they ever find that woman?"

I guess by then this shouldn't have surprised me. As much as I had asked friends, neighbors, and family members to stop pursuing the driver by offering rewards and putting up posters, they never really did. Next to "How's Grant?" the question I got asked the most was "Did they ever find the driver?" The answer was no. They hadn't. And I didn't care. The woman who had hit Grant was irrelevant to his progress, and therefore irrelevant to me. I tried not to give her a moment's thought and encouraged everyone around me to do the same.

One of our new attendees at that Mindshare was Jeff Hays, a serial entrepreneur and filmmaker. I had met Jeff at Joe Polish's event and was thrilled that he was joining us. Like so many of us in that room, Jeff had been through an unspeakable tragedy earlier in his life—the loss of a child.

At lunch, I sat next to Jeff and asked him more about his son Charlie. When Jeff had married Charlie's mother several years before, Charlie was seven and had already been diagnosed with a rare and terminal form of thyroid cancer. Jeff adopted Charlie, thinking that his role would be to support his wife through the death of her son. He never expected to come to love Charlie so deeply or for Charlie to love him too, but that's exactly what happened.

"I wasn't in a supporting role anymore," he told me. "I was in a leading role that I hadn't prepared for or thought through." Charlie lived for another five years. When he passed away in 1997, Jeff was tempted to withdraw from the world and wallow in his sadness. He dropped out of business and went back to college at the University of Utah. "On campus I saw a quote from Joseph Campbell," Jeff told me. " 'Participate joyfully in the sorrows of the world. We cannot cure the world of sorrows, but we can choose to live in joy.' " Jeff paused for a moment. "I read that quote over and over," he said. "It became my guidepost through this. It was a sorrowful moment, but I was determined to live in joy."

Jeff told me that he'd been able to withstand the pain of Charlie's passing by focusing on all the good things that had come from Charlie's young life. Being Charlie's father, even for a short time, had been one of the greatest joys of Jeff's life. While he would have chosen a longer life for Charlie for his sake, Jeff fully enjoyed each moment he had with his son, and he wouldn't have exchanged that for anything in the world.

When Charlie was alive, he had insisted on donating his body to science. His specific type of cancer was very rare, and he wanted to contribute to finding a cure. A doctor named Ruth Decker did research on Charlie and was able to identify the genetic marker for his type of thyroid cancer.

Years later, Jeff was reading a copy of *Men's Health* magazine when he came across a story about new genetic solutions to certain cancers that featured three men who had tested positive for the same type of thyroid cancer that had taken Charlie's life and had had their thyroids removed. This had saved all three of their lives.

"I was sitting there alone in my office looking at three men who wouldn't be alive if it wasn't for Charlie," Jeff told me. "A few years after Charlie died, his birth father had another son, and the genetic test showed that the boy had the gene," Jeff continued. "They removed his thyroid, and his father's too."

Jeff paused and smiled at me. "Because of Charlie, they were able to save his little brother and eventually his own father. He had a very impactful life."

I should have been inspired, but when I got home from the event, I felt lower than ever. The questions about the driver who had hit Grant and my conversation with Jeff both weighed on me. I felt like I was missing something. I thought I had moved on from the accident, but my mind kept going back there. Whenever I was alone, at work, or at the gym, I pictured the car hitting Grant. I imagined the woman, whom I'd never seen, standing over him and looking at his blood and bones before deciding to take off without even calling for help. I saw her in my dreams, laughing over Grant's broken body as he lay unconscious in the hospital bed.

I didn't understand why I kept thinking about this woman now, so many months after the accident. But I knew one thing—I wasn't participating joyfully in the sorrows of the world. I was holding on to anger and resentment, and it was crushing my joy.

When I woke up from another nightmare about the driver a few mornings later, I realized that I couldn't ignore her anymore. For so long, I had tried to just focus on Grant and forget about the woman who had done this to him, but she was a part of this story too. I couldn't keep pretending that she was irrelevant. But instead of seeking vengeance, I had to do something that no one expected me to do, especially not me. I had to actively forgive her.

I went into my home office and sat there in silence. I knew that the key to forgiving this woman would be in finding the gifts in Grant's accident, just like the way Jeff had managed to accept his son's death by focusing on all the good things that had come out of his short life. But first I had to unleash my true feelings about the driver. I had been stuffing them down for so long, but they had left scars. It was time to finally heal them.

I closed my eyes and pictured myself in a room with the driver. Though I didn't know what she looked like in real life, I imagined her in great detail, down to her pale pink fingernails and dark jeans. Then I pictured a judge. In my mind, it was the lion from Narnia, a big and powerful presence that could help us find justice.

"You hit my son," I said out loud. "You nearly killed him." I was charging her with her crimes, determined to let it all out and make the lion judge see it from my perspective. "And then you left him," I continued. "You didn't even get him help. He could have died before anyone else got there, and it would have been your fault."

I paused to make sure I had said everything I needed to say. I didn't feel quite done. "You treated him like his life didn't matter," I said finally. "But you don't have the power to decide."

I sat quiet for a moment and then went back into that courtroom in my mind. This time I tried to see things from the driver's perspective, as if I were pleading her case. The one thing I had always wondered was why she would leave him there. Instead of letting this question hang in the air any longer, I tried to finally answer it.

"I was scared to death," I said, playing the role of the driver. "I had two little kids at home, and I was afraid that I'd go to jail for the rest of my life. There would be no one to take care of them." I tried to feel her fear, imagining myself in that situation when my own boys were little. Who knows what I would have done if I were in her shoes?

Once I had seen things from her side, it was time to find the gifts this woman had given me. This part was easy. Before the accident, I had struggled for so long to be present with my kids, and now I was. I felt closer to my family and my friends than ever before. I had learned new things about myself, and I had grown.

As hard as the past year had been for both Grant and Bryce, it had also made them stronger. Bryce had been forced to fend for himself at the age of fifteen, and while a part of me felt guilty about this, it was easy to see that he had stepped up to the challenge and thrived. He was so much more mature than most kids his age, and the strength he'd gained from this experience would serve him well throughout his life. Nothing was going to throw him after this.

And Grant, well . . . Grant got his fresh start. Life wouldn't always be easy for him, but it wasn't easy before the accident either. Now he had softness, empathy, and a new spiritual side along with his creativity. While he hadn't quite found his place in the world yet, I was sure that he was on his way to discovering a bigger purpose than he'd ever thought possible. Simply knowing now that he was alive for a reason was an enormous gift. I'd witnessed how people reacted to seeing him in the flesh, how affected they were just by hearing his story. His life had a new meaning. It might have been daunting at times, but I had no doubt that he would eventually live up to the challenge.

I took a breath and pictured the lion looking at me with approval. I had finally forgiven her. I could feel it. But the unsettled feeling inside of me still lingered. It was as if I had cleaned my whole house, but there was a mess hiding beneath the carpet or behind the walls that I couldn't see but that I could feel. Maybe there was someone else I had to forgive.

After sitting with this feeling for a few weeks, I realized that it wasn't enough to just forgive the woman who had hit Grant. I had to forgive everyone involved in the accident. That meant forgiving Grant, and it also meant forgiving myself. Since the night of the accident, I had replayed our argument in my head over and over, asking myself how things might have been different if I had gone after Grant when he stormed out or if I'd just let him go to the martial arts class in the first place.

So I repeated this forgiveness exercise while putting myself on trial. First I accused myself of being a bad mom for letting him walk off in such a state, for not letting him to go martial arts, and even for coddling him too much when he was younger. I had always secretly feared that his outbursts were my fault.

Then I defended myself. I had shown up for Grant. I had done my best. That was all anyone could have asked of me. And the gifts I'd received from my role in the accident were invaluable. I was a better mother now—that I was sure of. I was also a better friend and a better leader. Not only had I learned to believe in myself more than ever, but I'd also learned to believe in all of me—the flaws and vulnerabilities along with the parts that were getting stronger.

Next it was time to forgive Grant. While he was in the coma, I wouldn't allow myself to question what his role was in the accident. I had to focus completely on getting him better. But it lurked there in the back of my mind. He had been so angry when he left that night. Was he being careless? Was it his fault? It felt good to finally unleash these thoughts and put them all out there as I accused Grant of all his possible wrongdoings.

Then I forced myself to see it from his perspective. He was still so young. His life must have often felt out of control. Once I really felt his confusion and his pain that night, I could finally let all of my anger and resentment go. Grant had given me so many gifts, both before and after the accident. He had forced me to stretch myself as a mother and allowed me to see the world from his unique perspective. As Jeff had said about his son's short life, I wouldn't have traded that for anything in the world.

My mind flashed to an image of Grant being zipped into his bed at Children's Hospital after he had lashed out at John. "I'm sorry, I'm sorry," he repeated, hunched over in bed as he rocked back and forth.

"I forgive you," I said out loud now, realizing I had never told Grant that before. I could almost feel the anger, the sadness, and the guilt lifting off me as I forgave him for everything—the trouble he'd caused John and me as a child, the argument the night of the accident. All of it was gone.

Over the next few weeks I felt like this simple process had shifted my whole perspective, making me aware of what was really behind my own feelings. When I got cut off in traffic one morning when I was already running late for a big meeting, my first instinct was to get angry. But as I quickly pivoted into seeing it from the other driver's perspective, I realized that I wasn't really angry with him. I was angry with myself for leaving the house late and putting myself in this situation. That other driver was just a scapegoat, and forgiving him immediately put me in a better mood.

As I practiced forgiving people for their missteps, I realized that I felt wronged in some way nearly every day. The choice of how to handle this was mine. I could allow a black tumor of hatred and resentment to grow inside me, or I could choose the peace that came with forgiveness. If I held on to hatred and anger, I would become a victim. I'd be handing my power over to someone else, usually someone whom I knew little or nothing about.

Hating and resenting other people wasn't going to make my life any better. In fact, it only made it worse. Finding the gifts I'd ultimately gotten from each person who wronged me was the only way to peacefully move forward. Without doing that, I'd constantly be stuck in the what-if cycle, wondering how things might have gone differently. By finding the gifts I'd received, I was able to see each slight as a good thing, and the what-ifs went away. I had finally discovered the final and perhaps most important element of the Miracle Mindset—forgiveness.

After doing the forgiveness exercise, I realized that I hadn't been suffering from post-traumatic stress; I had been depressed. But I wasn't anymore. The simple act of forgiveness had crushed that sadness. It was that powerful. This meant that choosing to forgive others for their wrongdoings, no matter how big or small, was the only way to gain power over my entire life.

This realization was incredibly empowering—so much so that I started to look at every area of my life where I felt even a shred of resentment to see if there was someone I could actively forgive. It didn't take very long for me to land on both of my mothers.

For me, growing up as an adopted kid was always difficult. My parents always told me the truth about my adoption, repeating the classic line that every adoptive parent uses: "We adopted you because you're so special." Even as a child, I didn't believe this for a second. If I was so special, I wondered, why did the most important people in my life decide to give me up?

It didn't help that I was so different in every possible way from my adoptive family. I was this six-foot-tall blond alien with entrepreneurial instincts and drive. My parents didn't know what to do with me, so I never felt that I got the support I needed. Our family dynamic was also complicated by the fact that my adopted brother, Brad, was schizophrenic. My parents had their hands full with him and left me to fend for myself while the space grew between us. We never had the close, loving relationship that I longed for. Eventually I stopped longing for the closeness that I thought I'd never get and put walls up around myself to protect me from what I was missing.

When I was in my twenties, I found my birth parents and learned that when my birth mother had had me, she was twenty-one and engaged to my birth father, who wanted to keep me. My mother decided to give me up even though she had support from my birth father and her own parents. This was crushing, because it meant that the family I believed I was meant to be with could have raised me. My mother was a scientist and my father an entrepreneur. They would have understood me, I thought. They would have known how to support and love me the way I needed. But instead of being with my birth family as I felt I should have been, I spent my first six weeks of life in a foster home before being adopted into the family that I never truly felt a part of.

The pain from this didn't hit me at full force until I had my own kids. Once I became a mom, I knew that someone would have to kill me to take my kids from me. While I wasn't a perfect mom, I did my best to understand my kids and made every effort to love and support them the way they needed. This made it all the more painful to realize that no one had ever done this for me.

I started the exercise with my birth mom, accusing her of being selfish, of abandoning me, and of sentencing me to life with a family I didn't belong with. Then I stepped to the other side and pictured myself at twenty-one—pregnant, scared, and not sure what to do. I thought about all the things my birth mother had done for me. She believed she couldn't give me what I needed, so she left her family and her fiancé in Eugene, Oregon, and went all by herself to a Catholic home for unwed mothers in San Francisco. When I was born, she fought to have me placed with the family that she thought was best. For the first time, I recognized the strength it had required for her to do that, and realized that this was the biggest gift she'd given me: her strength.

I moved on to my adoptive mom. Her crimes were not supporting me the way I needed growing up, disconnecting from me, and never making me feel like she truly loved me. But when I took her side, I felt her pain from not being able to have her own children and then adopting two kids and having one of them turn out to have big problems. For the first time, I could relate to the way she was forced to focus on my brother and leave me to take care of myself, which led to the distance that grew between us.

This was not unlike the dynamic between Grant and Bryce, especially after the accident, when Grant needed my undivided attention. As I vowed not to let the same distance grow between Bryce and me that had always existed between my mom and me, I could feel her pain of wanting to be close to me but not knowing how to make that happen.

Like Bryce, when I was forced to take care of myself at a young age, I stepped up and got stronger. This was one of the gifts my mom had given me. Another gift that came from being raised in that family was my ability to spot the earliest sign that there was something different about Grant. After growing up with a schizophrenic brother, I was able to recognize mental illness and take action right away.

After I forgave my mother, I started to feel guilty about our relationship, but this time when I checked in with myself, I could see that the guilt was warranted. When my father was dying from cancer, I had promised him that I was going to take care of my mom. He had lost seventy pounds and was confined to a hospital bed in the bedroom of my childhood home, and he wasn't letting go.

As I sat beside my dad, holding his hand, I told him, "Dad, you can let go. I've got this." But after he died, I didn't follow through on my promise. Over the past few years I hadn't spent much time with my mom at all because I was so full of anger and resentment.

It was time for that to change. As soon as I could take a break from work, I visited my mom and started an intervention to help her deal with my brother, who was still living at home and creating daily stress for her. For the first time, I felt nothing for her but compassion and love. It wasn't until I felt it that I realized how much it had been missing before. I had always been hurt and angry that she wasn't what I wanted her to be, and finally I understood why she was the way she was and could accept everything about her.

I got back from my visit in time for Mother's Day and went out to brunch with Bryce and Grant. Going out to eat was still our favorite thing to do together. I sat across from them, feeling like a completely new person. For the first time in my life, there was nothing weighing on me—no guilt, no resentment, and no fear. For months I had been telling myself that I would calm down when Grant finished high school, and then when he had a group of friends, and then when he gained more independence. I'd been looking at the horizon, but not anymore. I was finally happy to be exactly where I was in that moment. Forgiveness had set me free.

Forgiving both of my mothers had been nothing less than transformative. Now that I was aware of the gifts I'd received from each of them, I felt that I could finally accept everything that had happened in my life. Even more, I was grateful for every last bit of it, from being adopted by my family to Grant's accident. If it hadn't been for every step I'd taken on this journey, I probably never would have felt the need to do the forgiveness exercise. I might have never gotten to this exact point.

If I had been given the choice, would I have wanted Grant to go through all the pain he'd endured throughout the past year? Of course not. But had it taken Grant's almost dying to make me more present, open, vulnerable, accepting, and content, while he became more sensitive, empathetic, and kind? Maybe. And I wasn't going to take any of that for granted. I was filled with gratitude for where we were precisely at that moment.

I looked at Grant as he dug into his food with pleasure. He was alive. That alone was a miracle, but it wasn't enough. He had to keep pushing forward—not toward a finish line, but to simply be his personal best. That's all that any of us can do. He had to make the most of the journey, and my job was to help him find a way to inhabit his best possible life.

Part of forgiving him meant that I had to stop asking myself which parts of Grant's personality were him, what was the brain injury, and what was his bipolar disorder. I had to accept Grant for Grant. The way he was now was Grant—all of it. His more positive, empathetic attitude was Grant. The fact that he couldn't tolerate being around large groups of people and easily grew overstimulated was Grant. The way he still mixed up the letters R and S and laughed at himself when he did was Grant. His love of art, which didn't exist before the accident, was Grant. And the way he smiled now with his whole face was simply Grant. Grant was here, and he was wonderful.

There would always be something else to worry about, some other finish line to aim for. No matter how much I wanted to put the accident behind us, it would never truly be behind us. This was our life now. Instead of trying to move on from it, I had to start looking at the accident from a different perspective. Seeing the gifts we'd all received from it was a huge step in that direction.

As I was lost in thought, Grant and Bryce had been engaged in what looked like an intense conversation. I noticed that they had been spending more time together lately—watching movies, listening to music, or just talking. They were slowly developing their own relationship as brothers, and it was amazing to watch.

Bryce had also taught me so much about Grant. After years of struggling to get along with him, Bryce finally understood his brother fully in a way I was sure I never would. When Grant got stuck in a negative thought spiral, Bryce knew how to get him out of it by presenting him with alternatives. When Grant messed up, instead of berating him, Bryce asked deliberately, "What would be the best way to handle that next time?" He brought out the best in Grant every time, and watching this was teaching me how to do the same thing.

"What were you two talking about?" I asked Bryce when Grant got up a few minutes later to go to the bathroom. For their entire lives, most of their conversations had ended with slammed doors and hurt feelings, not the peaceful way they'd spoken today.

"We were just talking about life," Bryce said. He must have seen the look of surprise on my face. "We have a lot of important things to say to each other," he told me.

"Like what?" I asked, desperately trying to sound neutral. I knew that the best way to get my teenage son to stop sharing with me was to let him know how interested I was in what he was saying.

Bryce seemed to consider my question as he chewed a bite of his food. "We've walked different paths and learned different things," he told me. "And now we can share that information with each other." Bryce turned to look at me. His face was wide open. "We finally get each other," he told me. "Isn't that cool?"

We stood up as Grant got back to the table, and I put my arms around both of my sons, pulling them close to me. "Yes, honey," I said, closing my eyes as I kissed the tops of their heads. "It's pretty cool."

WARRIOR MOM'S MANTRA

When you let go of your hurt and anger, you make room for new hope. Life will bring disappointment, and people may let you down. But when moms choose to live in joy anyway, we show our families what it means to experience real freedom.

CONCLUSION:

You Are Stronger Than You Think You Are

Shortly after Mother's Day I was scheduled to speak at the California Women's Conference, the largest women's conference in the country. It was a huge event that I was very excited about, but as the date approached, I found that I didn't want to leave the boys. Ever since I had gone through the forgiveness exercise, I had been craving connection, whereas before I'd prided myself on my independence. The walls I had put up around me as a child had been torn down, and I wanted to be close to the people I loved, especially my sons. Bryce was busy with his friends, so I took Grant with me to the event.

Jack Canfield, the man behind *Chicken Soup for the Soul*, and I were the headline speakers at the event. Grant seemed excited about meeting Jack and hearing him speak. I still longed to find a way to show Grant that he had the potential to inspire just as many people as someone like Jack. Maybe this was my opportunity.

For a long time I'd believed that the only gifts we'd received from the accident were the changes in us. Both Grant and I were more patient, less easily rattled, and more vulnerable. My friends constantly told me that I was "softer around the edges." But the more I talked about our experience and saw the way people reacted, I realized that we'd gotten an even bigger gift—the opportunity to help others simply by sharing our story. Just hearing what we'd been through was beginning to help people shift their perspectives, allowing them to take on the Miracle Mindset that I now knew without a doubt had helped save Grant's life.

While some media outlets that covered Grant's story wanted to peg his recovery to one element of his treatment—the fish oil, the progesterone, the power of prayer, or the intense therapy— none of these things could be separated from the others. Yes, the fish oil had played a role. The massive prayer, the progesterone, and every bit of love and support that we surrounded Grant with had all played a role. But it was our mindset that played the biggest role.

The Miracle Mindset had allowed me to see every challenge we'd faced over the past year as an opportunity to flex my muscles and get stronger. It had forced me to be present in each moment and to focus on possibilities and hope rather than self-imposed limitations. It spurred me to take action every day, no matter how small or imperfect it may have been, while committing to greatness. It taught me how to be vulnerable and accept help from others, and perhaps most important, it had revealed the life-changing power of forgiveness.

Seeing this mindset begin to manifest itself in my colleagues from the Mindshare Summit, followers of *The Virgin Diet* and *JJ Virgin's Sugar Impact Diet*, and even friends and coworkers like Susan was the most rewarding thing I'd ever experienced. It made all the pain and suffering our family had gone through seem worth it. I would have given anything for Grant to feel this too.

Throughout my speech, which was mainly about *The Virgin Diet*, I implored the audience not to let their health hold them back. Using Grant's story as an example, I explained that they had to be ready for the good and the bad that life might throw at them, often without a moment to catch their breath. I taught them about the Miracle Mindset and explained how to use it to create amazing changes in their lives.

When I was finished speaking, I called Grant onto the stage. The thousands of women in the audience gave him a standing ovation. Grant and I held hands and took a bow, and as Grant walked offstage, Jack Canfield approached and gave him a fist bump and a big hug. Immediately after, I held a book signing. Grant was there next to me, and hundreds of women came up to him and asked for a hug. More women came over to see him than to get a book signed by me! But I didn't mind. One by one, as each woman embraced Grant, I could see that without even realizing it or intending to, Grant was giving them back their hope.

The look on Grant's face was priceless—awe, pride, and happiness all in one. Grant turned to face the women who'd gathered around him and raised his right arm in victory as he took in all the people he'd just inspired. I could see in his eyes then that he knew. He had a purpose. He had a reason to be here. And this was it.

This story isn't going to wrap up perfectly with a pretty bow. As I write this, it's been two years since that women's conference. The past two years have been full of ups and downs, challenges and miracles. For many months, we struggled to determine what Grant's next step should be. He wasn't happy at home, but he wasn't ready to move out on his own either. He needed a change in environment, but where? How?

Finally I found a place for him in Utah with a family who had a large property and a separate apartment for kids like Grant who need some help learning how to live independently. It was a big deal for me to let him move so far away from home. At that point, I still wasn't comfortable letting him cross the street by himself. But I realized that I couldn't keep holding on to him so tightly. I had to let him go and be free to make his own mistakes, get frustrated, and learn how to manage when things didn't go his way—just like everyone else.

In Utah, Grant was able to spend a lot of time outdoors. There were certain guidelines, but he was free to come and go as he pleased and could spend as much time as he liked with the family and their dog. For a few months, it seemed like the perfect fit. Sure enough, there were times when Grant called me frustrated, and there was nothing I could do. I was too far away to try to rescue him, and Grant had to learn to fend for himself.

After a few months, Grant moved into his own apartment and got a job working at a grocery store. I was nervous yet again to let him sink or swim, but he thrived there. The rest of the staff adored him, and Grant enjoyed making the customers smile. Knowing that he could make people happy and impact their lives just by being himself was huge for Grant. He was beginning to see that he had something valuable to offer.

When he moved back home just six months after leaving for Utah, Grant was calmer, happier, and far more self-sufficient than before. Instead of sitting around whining that he had no purpose, he started studying subjects that interested him, from philosophy and religion to hydroponics. After reading about it online, he turned our entire backyard into a huge hydroponic garden that he powered using a solar panel and a car battery. When he wasn't working on the garden, he was working out—sprinting, lifting weights, playing tennis, and fine-tuning his balance.

No matter how challenging his life may be at times or how much I still worry about him, which is plenty, I believe that today Grant is 110 percent. He is kinder, more positive, and determined not to be seen for his limitations. Grant is also different in profound ways that can't easily be explained. He's seen death. He survived for weeks at its edge, and this has given him a powerful new perspective on life.

Most important, Grant has seen the power of the Miracle Mindset. He knows that he can choose to be either a victor or a victim in life, and he is clearly a victor. Grant has never once asked why this happened to him or seen himself as a victim when he so easily could have. Instead, he has taken full responsibility for where he is going from here and is willing to put in the necessary work every day to keep getting better. He personifies the Miracle Mindset, and I know that it will get him exactly where he's meant to go.

I may have been the first one to say that the accident was going to be the best thing that ever happened to Grant, but I didn't make that prediction come true—he did. And watching Grant fight his way from the brink of death to become the stronger yet gentler and more loving person he is today has taught me that this is possible for anyone. No matter what you're facing or how many blows life deals you, no one can make you a victim without your permission.

Grant has made his journey one of victory, and the best thing we can do now is pass that torch on to you. The process of writing this book has helped me heal from the pain and trauma of almost losing my son, so thank you for reading it and giving me that opportunity. Thank you for helping Grant find his purpose by letting him inspire you, and thank you for picking up that torch and running with it. No matter what obstacles may lie ahead, we can keep going knowing that you've benefited from our story.

Now it's your turn to work those muscles and start getting stronger so that you're ready to lean into whatever challenges and opportunities life has in store for you. Don't wait for miracles; go out and make them. You are stronger than you think.

LIVE FIERCE!

Get the support and tools you need to step up every day at www.WarriorMomBook.com/resources.

Gratitude

First, I want to thank you for joining me on this journey. Writing this book has been quite an emotional process. It required me to relive the most painful, scary, and desperate moments of my life. But as I remembered the tough parts, I was also reminded of how many people it took to bring Grant back from almost dying to thriving. This was very healing.

There are many people I clearly remember, as well as many others whose names I don't even know. I am grateful to all of you: the neighbor who stopped the night of the accident, protected Grant from getting hit again, and called 911. All the first responders, including the paramedics and the Palm Desert police who fought for my son's life. The medical team at Desert Regional Medical Center, who performed emergency lifesaving techniques that allowed Grant to make it to Harbor-UCLA. Susan Tafralis, who talked me off the ledge that night at the hospital, not to mention the many times before and after that!

I call Dr. Carlos Donayre Grant's angel. You saved Grant's life twice and were extraordinarily kind and patient. The doctors and nurses at Harbor-UCLA went far beyond the call of duty. It was obvious that this is so much more than a job to you; it is your mission. Isis Tello, you are an extraordinary nurse and human being. You helped me stay hopeful in the darkest hours. Thank you to Dr. Kevan Craig for accepting Grant at Children's Hospital Los Angeles. You and your amazing team were instrumental in Grant's rapid progress.

Being in a hospital setting for months at a time is a difficult, emotionally draining experience, but I was fortunate to have amazing support first from my younger son, Bryce, and the boys' incredibly patient father, John. Then there was literally a village of people who showed up to help us with everything from homemade chicken soup to essential oils to dark chocolate. Thank you to Dr. Hyla Cass, Dr. Prudence Hall, Dr. Daniel and Tana Amen, Dr. Susanne Bennett, Dr. Anne Meyer, Dr. Allen and Jeanne Peters, Dr. Hooman Fakki, Dr. Joan Rosenberg, Grace Suh, Dorcey Russell, and everyone who sent us supplies, love, and prayers, including Dr. Alan Christianson, Dr. Sara Gottfried, Allen Ting, Leanne Ely, Todd Parker, Betsy Foster and the Whole Foods Gang, Randy Hartnell and Vital Choice Seafood, Dr. Stephen Sinatra, and Tommy Rosa.

Big thanks to those of you who helped me quickly track down the latest brain trauma research and protocols: Dr. Anna Cabeca, Dr. Donald Stein, Dr. Robert Rountree, Dr. Barry Sears, and Dr. Michael Lewis. Thank you to the forward-thinking media professionals who brought this story into the daylight early on: the team at *The Doctors*, Dr. Sanjay Gupta at CNN, and Dr. Joe Mercola at www.mercola.com.

The heavy lifting for us really started when we got Grant home.

John, thank you for playing the leading role here. We are both grateful for the amazing help we received from Grant's speech therapist, Marcey Utter, and his conditioning coach, Michael Butler of Kinetix. Thank you to Leslie Locken, who orchestrated a community fund-raiser for Grant before she even met us! And most of all, thank you, Grant, for never being a victim, for staying positive, and for looking to consistently improve while finding ways to help others.

Of course this all went down during the craziest time in my business, but I had support from an amazing team and great mentors. Brendon Burchard, thank you for going way beyond the call of duty to help ensure that *The Virgin Diet* succeeded. Thanks to my amazing agent, Celeste Fine, for not only stepping in to help out with *The Virgin Diet*, but for making sure I kept the momentum going with *The Virgin Diet Cookbook*, *JJ Virgin's Sugar Impact Diet*, and *JJ Virgin's Sugar Impact Diet Cookbook* and then insisting that I take on this project and get Grant's story out to the world.

Ellyne Lonergan, you've been instrumental in helping me get all my stories out as my public television producer for *The Virgin Diet* and *The Sugar Impact Diet* and now as my documentary producer for *You're Stronger Than You Think*.

I would have crumbled through this process if it hadn't been for the amazing writing support from Jodi Lipper. Jodi, you are pure magic and a genius.

Getting this book out along with all the supporting podcasts, blogs, social media, and videos is a monumental job, and I have the A team that does it. I am so honored to work with Susan Tafralis, Chris Groutt, Karl Krummenacher, Kim Ward, Oliver Waller,

Spring Barnickle, Carole Lehmann, Rick Dilliott, Mary Ann Guillory, Brandy Burke, Travis Houston, Leslie Sciratt, Jennifer Vega, Nadiya Gillani, Rose Curran, and Melanie Humphrey.

To my style gals: photography whisperer Leslie Boehm and the amazing makeup artist Tamara Ogden. I won't do a cover without you!

Michele Martin, thank you for being one of the first people to see the vision for this book and for believing in me. I couldn't have done it without you. Sophia Muthuraj, thank you for your insights that helped make this book as good as it could be. And a huge thank you to the entire team at North Star Way for using your talents to help bring this book to life.

Finally, thank you, Mom, for helping me become the strong woman I am today. And to my partner, my best friend, and the love of my life, Tim O'Horgan, I am so grateful for your support, guidance, and patience. I'm glad you enjoy a bit of chaos!

Artwork by Grant Virgin